BEAUTY
AND THE EAST

gestalten

WE ARE RUNNING TOWARD A NEW WORLD OF UNCERTAINTY
跑向一个不确定的新世界

A foreword by Wang Shu

There is probably not a single Chinese architect who has not become a devotee of modern architecture after studying French master Le Corbusier's collection of essays *Vers une Architecture* (*Towards a New Architecture*, 1927). It's interesting to note that the translated Chinese title "走向新建筑" (Zouxiang Xin Jianzhu) also carries the meaning of "moving firmly toward a goal, step by step." The reality in China, however, is that new buildings are in such urgent demand that urbanization is increasing at a rate unprecedented in the history of the world. If these dazzling changes have anything in common, it is the pursuit of "novelty." Simply putting up more buildings is clearly not satisfying any sector of society, from the general public to the government. People seem desperate to abandon the status quo and are crying out for their cities to be refashioned. There are over 110 cities with a population of more than a million and about 3,000 with a population of more than 300,000. Many of these cities are more than a thousand years old, and they are all determinedly moving toward the "new world." One doesn't need precise statistics to see that in the past 30 years, at least 90 percent of these buildings—which had been built and maintained in traditional Chinese style, encapsulating cultural values—have been demolished. Now it seems more of a sprint than a mindful march to the new world. But what is this "new world"? There is probably no definite answer because it has been changing every few years, and it is, by nature, uncertain. What is certain is that everything keeps changing, and change is what people crave.

But there are growing concerns about the new architecture and cities among the general public in China. In the 1990s people were mainly concerned about the newness of cities and buildings; after 2000 they started paying attention to their quality. Also, in the 1990s, architects were seen as a collective, and it was only in the new millennium that outstanding architects started to be recognized individually. Despite this, and even though China has the largest number of new buildings in the world, most of them are merely imitations of the existing ones; and they are so crudely built that they are just like piles of concrete garbage. Why are there so few good buildings? Good buildings with Chinese cultural characteristics? Why does almost every city seem to look the same? In Chinese, we call it "千城一面" (qian cheng yimian) "a thousand cities with one face." And, why are all villages, once so rich and diverse, becoming identical? These questions have been gradually causing anxiety, from the ground up to the government.

A DEARTH OF GOOD BUILDINGS?

Public opinion varies. I remember that around 2000, the best answer the architectural community could give to the question of why there was a dearth of good buildings in China, was: "Everything is changing so fast, we are not ready yet." But not long after 2000, a small group of young Chinese architects began to attract the attention of the media; their creativity, criticality, and personal characteristics generated truly original work. Among this group of authentic minds, I remember the most eagerly shared concern was how to improve the quality of building construction. These architects are obviously ideological and exploratory by nature, but the inadequacy of construction quality has been an arduous challenge, which culminated in a movement emphasizing the research of materials and construction. From today's perspective, this seemingly inconsequential focus has had a profound impact →

→ on the exploration of new Chinese architecture in the past two decades because it grasps the fundamental shortcomings of the professional systems and habits of Chinese architects.

Until the end of the 1990s, there were essentially no independent architectural practices in China as the state-owned mega design institutes dominated the field of architecture and design. More often than not, these institutes tended to be caught between functionalism and changes in architectural styles. By and large, they operated as design factories. Before long, these institutes were drawn into a whirlpool of large-scale developments—the number of projects was giddying, and the requests relentless; coupled with this was the persistent demand from the state, where assessment of its development progress urgently required a large quantity of new buildings. In such conditions, it was almost impossible to produce good architecture.

MORE PROJECTS, MORE OPPORTUNITY

On the plus side, the large number of projects created opportunities for a generation of architects and ensured the survival of independent practices. There was a plea from the architecture scene to encourage the establishment of independent architectural practices, which were commonly agreed to be effective in improving the quality of architectural design. A number of architects set up their own studios in the 1990s. Although it has been an effort to survive, these architects share a passion for forging a path to more thoughtful, artistic, and critical architecture. In truth, the reason why good buildings are difficult to produce is not so much that the architects are not ready, but rather, faced with the temptation of a large number of projects, they need to exercise great judgment and self-discipline to opt for quality over quantity. At the same time, in the face of the distorted reality of this abnormal development, an intelligent, holistic approach to operations and quality control is required.

Interestingly, regardless of their size, big institutes and independent practices face the same challenges. An architectural design proposal, for instance, conventionally takes half a year from field investigation through schematic concept to design development. A Chinese client, however, whether it be a private enterprise or the government, for whatever reason, will allow only two months, so things always proceed in feverish haste.

In the 1990s people were mainly concerned about the newness of buildings; after 2000 they started paying attention to their quality. In the 1990s, architects were seen as a collective, and it was only in the new millennium that outstanding architects started to be recognized individually.

Western civilization has completely entered the modern stage of artificialization, but China is still in a period of transition between a traditional society close to nature and a modern, highly artificial industrialized society.

And, while it typically takes a further six months to finish construction drawings, in China, architects are usually granted just two months, and very often, drawings are rendered without a thoroughgoing design proposal. In truth, most constructions in China start before the completion of the drawings to meet the performance assessment cycles. I have always been impressed by how skillful these big institutes are in managing to complete the drawings from rough design proposals, but it explains why fastidious architectural critics always find fault with new buildings. The attitude seems to be: if a window is missing, just send a builder to chisel one in; if there is an extra one, just block it up. Switches and sockets are always in the wrong place and slightly askew—all because everything was designed and constructed in a hurry. It has even come to the point where people are starting to believe that roughcast spaces are how new buildings are supposed to be and that further alterations and decoration to complete them are the responsibility of the end users.

THE RISE OF INDEPENDENT PRACTICES

Nowadays, our society possesses higher standards of architecture (or should I say it has improved), but there haven't been any fundamental changes. The architects of these design institutes are extremely industrious, as clients are in a position to negotiate down the design fee and pressure them with even tighter deadlines. So why do they work so hard? Is it to secure a higher income? Perhaps we could say that whether a design is good or bad depends entirely on the architect's conscience and self-discipline in implementing their creative and professional ideals. In such circumstances, one can imagine that most of the excellent contemporary architecture that has risen from the chaos of this rapid development is by independent practices and small studios run by architects who have made extraordinary efforts and maintained control over their own particular operating strategies. This requires a level of idealism, and I believe that all of these brilliant Chinese architects are quite idealistic.

Apart from the design, construction is an equally decisive factor in determining the quality of a building. Architects often complain that the technical capability of Chinese builders—especially migrant workers from rural areas—is too low. This is the reality we face. Excluding a few special projects, migrant workers make up a large part of the construction workforce for most of the country's public buildings, yet most of them have never received even basic modern-day technical training. I often notice that they can't even perform cast-in-place concrete—a common technique where the concrete is poured on-site—precisely. In one of our large-scale rammed-earth building projects, "瓦山" (Tiles Hill) at the China Academy of Art in Hangzhou, the concrete pillars inside were not aligned correctly. The special textures of many of the materials developed by our studio were created in the process of correcting errors on-site. For example, when concrete for a wall was poured into a honeycomb-pitted surface, I encouraged the workers to chisel it further to turn it into a feature. Then I discovered that they could handle concrete in the same way as traditional stone-carving artisans.

Many migrant workers are masters of certain traditional crafts, from which we can see how critical craftsmanship was to the building of traditional Chinese houses in the countryside and where the roots of Chinese culture lie and are strengthened. For Chinese architects, this presents a remarkable opportunity for creativity. Western civilization has completely entered the modern stage of artificialization, but China is still in a period of transition between a traditional society close to nature and a modern, highly artificial industrialized society. Rediscovering the value of traditional craftsmanship may lead the way to a unique new world of sustainable development. Architects who do not understand this are foolish.

REASSESSING THE VALUE OF THE TRADITIONAL

The debates of the younger generation of architects in the late 1990s were not simply about materials and construction; in contrast to the prevalent postmodern decorative style of that time, they were more concerned with purifying the language of architecture itself, exploring the logic of space and excluding any irrelevant or unnecessary expressions. It was less about architectural concepts and more about reassessing the value of the traditional Chinese construction system in the contemporary environment. Inevitably, these continuing discussions are influenced by the popular language of world architecture—many Chinese architects pursue a new sense of form, texture, and space; sometimes this is presented in a coating of natural landscape and ecology, at other times it is rationalized with traditional Chinese art. Although I worked on a series of renovations and reuse projects in the 1990s, where

Judging by today's focus on the sustainability of future construction practices, the Chinese traditional construction system, in which architecture is dominated by natural materials, is actually ahead of its time; it is simultaneously traditional and fit for the future.

The unavoidable reality is that the construction system in Chinese cities today has been almost completely modernized. For our traditions to survive, it is necessary to find a way for the two systems to coexist, and since 2000 this has been one of the most important tasks for Amateur Architecture Studio.

the common notion was to create a dialogue between the old and the new—an experience that has profoundly influenced our work at Amateur Architecture Studio—it was in the ruins of traditional cities where I really gained a more profound understanding of materials and construction. In 2000, the biggest demolition of traditional neighborhoods took place in Hangzhou, the city where I lived. Lu Wenyu and I sculpted a small work using recycled building materials for the very first time for an international sculpture exhibition in the city. I realized that this 1,000-year-old city, once praised by Marco Polo as the most beautiful in the world, was rapidly losing its memory.

Architecture—and building materials in particular—carry people's memories and their cultural identity. Not only that, judging by today's focus on the sustainability of future construction practices, the Chinese traditional construction system, in which architecture is dominated by natural materials, is actually ahead of its time; it is simultaneously traditional and fit for the future. The vandalism of traditional architecture in Chinese cities is an incomprehensible tragedy. People are destroying their own future with their own hands.

The unavoidable reality is that the construction system in Chinese cities today has been almost completely modernized; concrete and steel are mainstream, together with the technologies and methods that have evolved with them. For our traditions to survive, it is necessary to find a way for the two systems to coexist, and since 2000 this has been one of the most important tasks for Amateur Architecture Studio. It is promising that there has been a general consensus among Chinese cities for the preservation of historical spaces—although it might have come too late. However, it is gratifying to see many young architects and small studios working on small, focused projects that contribute to the repurposing and regeneration of the architecture and traditional neighborhoods, in both urban and rural areas.

Perhaps, we can now finally catch a hazy glimpse of what our future could be. ∎

WANG SHU

is a Chinese architect, partner in Amateur Architecture Studio with Lu Wenyu, and a professor at the Academy of Art in Hangzhou. Wang became the first Chinese citizen to win the Pritzker Prize, the world's most prestigious architectural award, in 2012.

BUILDING AT AN UNPRECEDENTED SCALE

The past, present, and future of Chinese architecture by Yoko Choy Wai-Ching

Over the last few decades, China has witnessed an architectural experiment on a scale never seen before. The country's astounding growth over the last forty years has brought with it unprecedented change in the built landscape, and it's not slowing down anytime soon. China's fast-evolving needs continue to expand to accommodate domestic migration and facilitate international trade, and these changes aren't just happening in existing cities; entire metropolises are being built from scratch.

Architects from the West are attracted to China's infinite possibilities to indulge their imagination. At the same time, local Chinese talents, some already celebrated domestically and others on their way up, have tremendous opportunities to make their mark on the nation's landscape.

Just 15 years ago, the only modern form of architecture in China were high-rise buildings. When people spoke about "Chineseness," they meant traditional and classical; there was no such thing as a modern interpretation or a new Chinese language. In 2012, Wang Shu received the Pritzker Architecture Prize, and four years later, Zhang Ke won the Aga Khan Award for Architecture. The international acclaim gained by such prestigious recognition, together with the practices featured in this volume helped to set the tone of China's new wave, securing its place on the international architectural scene.

EXPANDING URBANIZATION

Urbanization in China began to accelerate following the initiation of the Chinese Economic Reform in 1978. The inflow of foreign investment generated massive employment opportunities in the nation's coastal regions, while rural towns further inland were urbanized as a result of industrialization driven by government policies, giving way to tremendous urban population growth. Architects seeking to find their identity within the Chinese cultural framework are doing so against a backdrop of prodigious modernization.

Newcomers to the country are amazed that such immense projects are approved and built at seemingly breakneck speed. One construction company claims to be the world's fastest builder after erecting a 57-story skyscraper in just 19 days (although, admittedly, it did spend four and a half months fabricating the building's 2,736 modules before construction began). Indeed, the country's global financial hub, Shanghai, and the entire city of Shenzhen, dubbed by the media "China's Silicon Valley," took a mere four decades to realize, providing us with a glimpse of the enormous possibilities to come.

Just a few figures suffice to illustrate the scale of recent development and demonstrate what is expected in the near future. In the last 70 years, the number of cities in China has risen from less than 60 to 672[1], and more than 60 percent of the population lives in urban areas today compared to just under 11 percent in the 1940s. Over the next decade or two, China's urban population is estimated to increase by more than a billion; that is more than the total number of people living in all the world's cities a century ago. By some estimates, almost half of the world's construction will take place in China in the coming decade (the country already builds 22 billion square feet (2 billion square meters) of new floor space each year—if it was laid out flat, that would be 1.3 times the size of the entire footprint of London)[2]; and in the 21st century, China might build more urban fabric than humanity has ever built before. →

THE STATE-OWNED DESIGN INSTITUTES

Since 1949, when the People's Republic of China was founded, architecture has been largely controlled by some 2,000 design institutes owned by the state or under its supervision. These institutes are responsible for overseeing the state's need for rapid large-scale infrastructural and architectural construction.

In the early days, design institutes operated with little to no competition. After the Economic Reform, the country gradually opened up, and overseas contractors and consultants were allowed to work in the country as it prepared to join the World Trade Organization, which it did in 2001. This poses opportunities and challenges for local design institutes. On the one hand, any firm entering the market needs to work with a local design institute, which in turn acquires new ideas, know-how, and methodologies from the West. On the other hand, there is increasing competition from the growing number of local independent practices that have emerged since the 1990s.

The establishment of individually run studios by leading in-house architects within design institutes is encouraged to ensure that they retain their competitive advantage and market influence. For example, Beijing Institute of Architectural Design (BIAD) is a large organization with a workforce of some 3,000 people but includes many boutique studios with a few dozen employees. Today's design institutes are, therefore, better equipped to fulfill the dual role of adhering to the traditional values of the nation's political regime while at the same time pursuing innovation and personal expression.

The symbiotic yet delicate relationship between private practices and state-owned institutes is pushing Chinese contemporary architecture development forward, according to Zeng Qun, chief architect of Tongji Architectural Design, who also leads his own design studio, "It is a crucial topic for architects on how to integrate architecture with contemporary society. Integration comes first, and then we start to talk about individuality and creativity, and about ourselves.

A further example of an acclaimed building by a state-owned design institute: the Beijing Phoenix Center by BIAD.

It is difficult and yet important to keep a social perspective. And Chinese architects, especially those in the big design institutes, have always borne this in mind."[3]

THE EXPERIMENTAL GENERATION

The dramatic social and political transformations that characterized China's economic reform were also the roots of an experimental phase in its architectural development that first emerged in the early 1990s. This prompted the growth of privately-operated Chinese architectural firms, which soon stole the spotlight by receiving acclaim from academia, the media, and the public alike.

Independent practices such as Atelier FCJZ (founded in 1993 in Beijing), Amateur Architecture Studio (founded in 1998 in Hangzhou), and Jiakun Architects (founded in 1999 in Chengdu), among others, are some of the most celebrated names in the movement. These practices do not share a common design philosophy; on the contrary, the members come from all over the country and some studied or practiced abroad and brought their ideas and techniques with them. What unites them is the goal of abandoning conventional ideologies to find a new "Chinese identity" for contemporary architecture.

This does not mean abandoning tradition for the sake of it. A significant aspect of contemporary Chinese architecture involves rediscovering and reworking existing ways of building. For example, Luo Studio employed prefabricated wooden structures in their design for the Party and Public Service Center of Yuanheguan Village in 2019 (p. 158), which responded to strict building and financial constraints and they delivered a scheme sympathetic to the surrounding Wudang Mountain area. Similarly, Amateur Architecture Studio's Ningbo Historic Museum, completed in 2008 (p. 286), is a masonry structure that features one of the studio's signature methods of creating building surfaces using traditional techniques and →

The China Pavilion for the World Expo 2010 in Shanghai offers an example of an acclaimed building designed by a state-owned design institute, headed by He Jingtang.

By some estimates, almost half of the world's construction will take place in China in the coming decade; and in the 21st century, China might build more urban fabric than humanity has ever built before.

The dramatic social and political transformations that characterized China's economic reform were also the roots of an experimental phase in its architectural development.

LUO Studio's Party and Public Service Center in Yuangeguan Village in Hubei Province, a new community center built using leftover foundations from an abandoned construction site.

→ reclaimed construction materials. "We must not demolish history in order to develop," Wang warns.

There is a growing emphasis on heritage preservation and objection to the demolition of historical landmarks, traditional architecture, and even ancient landscapes from both the state officials and independent practices. It is here that local knowledge will come into its own as more insightful practitioners withstand the temptation to build incongruously showy buildings as vanity projects. The merits of architectural preservation came to public attention with Atelier Deshaus's Long Museum (West Bund) project in 2014 (p. 262), which demonstrates a carefully considered retrofit design, retaining the appearance of the wharf originally built for coal transportation of the 1950s with the addition of a series of intersecting vaulted cantilever structures. More recently, Open Architecture's Tank Shanghai, finished in 2019, transformed five decommissioned aviation fuel tanks on a dilapidated industrial site into a cultural park and multifunctional art space, earning much international praise.

Since the imprudent demolition that occurred in the lead up to the 2008 Olympics, there have been numerous projects designed to rejuvenate Beijing's historic neighborhoods called *hutongs* and the traditional courtyard houses, known as *siheyuan*. In order to stem the tide of destruction, research into new social and economic models for the city's development agenda is being undertaken to create an ecosystem that fits the needs of modern city life. Twisting Courtyard by ARCHSTUDIO completed in 2017 (p. 188) proposed a new relationship between indoor and outdoor living; Urbanus's No.37 Luanqing Hutong (p. 184), completed in the same year, involved renovating the traditional, vernacular layout and historical features to create a unique spatial experience.

Beyond the major cities, the government is keen to avoid neglecting the nation's rural life and is allocating funds to ensure that villages are not abandoned in the process of urbanization. While many developing countries see their rural populations stampeding to the cities, China is considering the wider picture and has ambitious schemes to make the best use of its vast territory. The Xiafu Village Farmers' Market by Bengo Studio in 2018, for instance, resulted from a series of investigations into the villagers' use of the market and an analysis of the social situations in such environments. For the Capsule Hotel and Bookstore in the ancient village of Qinglongwu (p. 138), deep in the forest, Atelier tao+c regenerated an old wooden structure to create a boutique hotel and community library, combining social benefits for the locals with the economic opportunity brought by tourism.

THE FUTURE OF CHINESE ARCHITECTURE

With all eyes on China, the architectural world is looking for an identity that defines this new body of work. Wang Yun, director of the Beijing University of Civil Engineering and Architecture Graduate School of Architecture Design and Art, founder of Atelier Fronti, says, "Unlike in Europe and the United States, which have their own cultural styles, Chinese architecture is evolving. We are in the process of transitioning to a stable style, which gives rise to diverse styles that are necessary for reaching a consensus in the future. We cannot criticize this; it may be chaos, but we need to for it to happen, to look at it rationally and discover its pattern and future."[4]

In 2014, President Xi Jinping famously called for an end to what he calls "weird architecture." This comment was prompted by the painful sight of a group of outrageous buildings with obvious foreign influences that had sprung up in mainland cities, bypassing accepted national tastes. Beijing's China Central Television headquarters (known as the "Giant Underpants"), designed by the Netherland's OMA in 2012, and British firm RMJM's 2016 Gate to the East in Suzhou (nicknamed "Low-rise Jeans") are two of the most controversial cases to date. President Xi's views were extended in a directive →

The Long Museum West Bund by Atelier Deshaus in Shanghai, a carefully considered retrofit design.

The architecture of revitalizing China's rural hinterland: Atelier tao+c's Capsule Hotel and Bookstore.

Atelier tao+c's Capsule Hotel and Bookstore in Zhejiang Province retained the structure's original timber frame and mud walls.

→   issued a year later by the State Council, which commanded that urban architecture be "suitable, economic, green, and pleasing to the eye," in contrast to the "oversized, xenocentric, peculiar" developments that had previously been constructed. Five years later, the country's Ministry of Housing and Urban-Rural Development and National Development and Reform Commission issued a circular with directions for the "new era" of city development. It prohibited buildings of more than 1,640 feet (500 meters), extending the skyscraper limits that were already in place in some cities, such as Beijing, along with "copycat" buildings. Instead, it instructed architects to design buildings that encapsulate China's character and respect their surroundings.

The state's agenda will remain the deciding factor in the direction of the country's development. President Xi's personally endorsed Xiong'an will probably be the next world-class metropolis. An urban innovation zone labeled as a "new standard in the post-pandemic era" located about 80 miles (130 kilometers) south-west of the capital will be an archetype that can also be applied elsewhere in the world. Unlike most mega-cities today, which are dominated by real estate speculators and tall, showpiece buildings, Xiong'an suggests a new paradigm for China's development. This self-sufficient neighborhood coincides with the national policy of using cutting-edge technology such as artificial intelligence, the Internet of Things, and next-generation 5G mobile networks. The project is expected to follow President Xi's proclamation at the UN General Assembly in September 2020 that China aims to start reducing carbon emissions before 2030 and be carbon neutral by 2060. Occupying 772 square miles (2,000 square kilometers)—almost as big as Greater London and New York combined—the city is scheduled for completion in 2035.

It is certainly not just China's politicians, planners, and architects who are considering how to make the country a model for the future built environment. "Probably the most important conversation that should happen today is about Asian cities, and especially Chinese cities," says Italian architect Carlo Ratti, director of Massachusetts Institute of Technology Senseable City Lab and co-curator of Bi-City Biennale of Urbanism/Architecture in Shenzhen 2019[5], a timely appraisal of the correlation between urbanization and technology innovation.

As Asia rises, breaking the West's domination of the world over the last few centuries, the scale of China's territory and the riches wrought by rapid modernization pave the way for the country to lead the way in 21st-century architecture and global development. Showcasing urban and rural expansion in a sustainable way that is appropriate yet unashamedly modern and proudly Chinese is a tall order—but one that its talented architects are eager and ready to fulfill. ∎

YOKO CHOY WAI-CHING

is a design writer and creative consultant, based in both Amsterdam and her native Hong Kong, who focuses on cross-cultural initiatives. She is the China editor of *Wallpaper** magazine and her work to date has been published in numerous Chinese and international titles.

1   People's Republic of China National Bureau of Statistics.

2   ZHANG Cici. "The country building a 'new London' every year," BBC, June 12, 2020, https://www.bbc.com/future/article/20200610-how-china-can-cut-co2-emissions-with-sustainable-buildings

3   ZHANG Yifan. "Conceiving Present Day of Future: A Talk with Zeng Qun," Archdaily, August 31, 2019, https://www.archdaily.com/923920/conceiving-present-day-of-future-a-talk-with-zeng-qun

4   LIU Shuang. "Architecture China 1000 Fang Zhenning's 21st Century Chinese Contemporary Architecture Cases Summary Exhibition (建筑中国1000方振宁的21世纪中国当代建筑案例总结展)," Artron, January 17, 2016, https://news.artron.net/20160117/n810635.html

5   Rima Sabina AOUF. "'China is one of the best places for experimenting' with urban technology says Carlo Ratti," Dezeen, April 25, 2019, https://www.dezeen.com/2019/04/25/carlo-ratti-interview-china-smart-cities-urban-technology-shenzhen-biennale/

There is a growing emphasis on heritage preservation and objection to the demolition of historical landmarks, traditional architecture, and even ancient landscapes.

DESIGNER	Amateur Architecture Studio
PROJECT	Sanhe Residence
LOCATION	Sifang Art Park, Nanjing

A Contemporary Celebration of Chinese Tradition in a 21st-Century Art Park

Nestled in a forested valley on the outskirts of Nanjing, the ancient capital of Jiangsu Province, Sifang Art Park, established in 2003, is home to a collection of 20 buildings designed by leading architects of the time, including New Yorker Steven Holl and Ghanaian-British David Adjaye. The concept arose as a backlash to the formulaic architecture of rapid urbanization in China's major cities and sought to showcase the best of 21st-century architecture and design. Among the buildings, Sanhe Residence was designed by Wang Shu of Amateur Architecture Studio. *Sanhe* translates roughly as "three-sided dwelling," and the abode is this architect's interpretation of the traditional Chinese courtyard house, known as *siheyuan*. In keeping with tradition, three volumes flank a central courtyard, in this case, with a reflecting pool at its center. The two residential volumes face one another across the courtyard, bridged by a third volume. Its glass facade looks out onto the interior courtyard at one end, and a series of repeating geometric openings at the rear overlook the forest. This volume houses the stairs that lead to the upper levels. Up above, a concrete canopy drapes over the three volumes, unifying them in a style that echoes traditional Chinese architecture. ▮

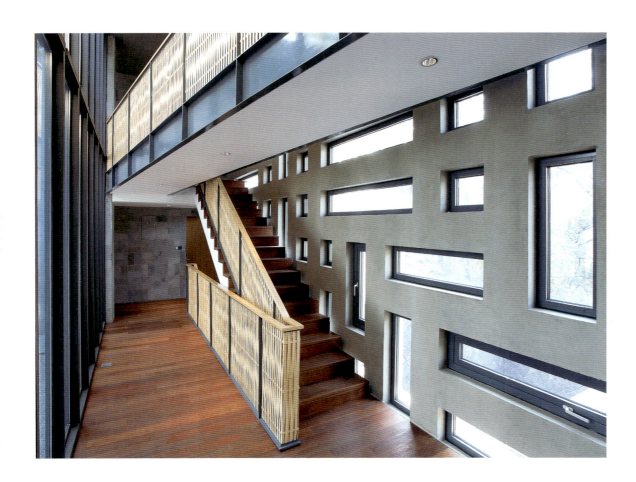

← Looking through from the internal courtyard to the art park beyond the house.

↙ The narrow bridging volume features an external wall of windows and a wall of glass overlooking the courtyard.

↓ The concrete canopy, while echoing the form of traditional Chinese dwellings, also has practical uses for drainage and shading.

Despite the use of concrete on a monumental scale, the house nestles comfortably into the surrounding landscape.

BIGGER, DENSER, AND MORE POPULOUS: DEVISING HOUSING SOLUTIONS AMID RAPIDLY GROWING CITIES

Urbanization has erected countless new buildings and demolished old towns, prompting contemporary Chinese architects to develop solutions that transcend the dilemma between old and new.

In 2013, residents of Beijing's Dashilan neighborhood were confronted with an unusual approach to urban regeneration. A series of futuristic sheet-metal prefabricated modules had been inserted into the central courtyard of a traditional *siheyuan* house as part of a pilot regeneration scheme. The Courtyard House Plug-In by People's Architecture Office (PAO) is designed to bring modern living standards and energy efficiency to the charming but old-fashioned homes, revitalizing the historic neighborhood in a simple, cost-effective way. The imagination demonstrated in creative residential architecture like this hints at a smarter future of housing in China, and contrasts with the usual "demolish and rebuild" model, which has been the driving force of China's urbanization for decades.

Modern China's housing revolutions can be divided into two phases: the socialist welfare housing built between 1949 and 1976, and the reform and neo-liberalization from 1977 to the present. From the outset of the socialist era, housing in China experienced a gradual transition from private rental to public rental and work-unit ownership. At the time, housing allocation policies required workers to be employed by public sector employers (work units), start families, and accumulate years of work. In the post-socialist era, following far-reaching reform and the opening-up initiated in 1978, private family homeownership became the norm. By 2007, a market-dominated home-owning urban society in China had begun to take shape.

In the first years of the 21st century, the momentum of decades of economic reforms culminated in China's pre-Olympic economic boom, but, since 2008, rapid urbanization and mass migration into major cities led to soaring house prices and widespread discontent. Taking Shanghai as an example, the average house price per square foot tripled from 2007 to

↑ The Courtyard House Plug-In is a prefabricated modular system for urban regeneration.

← Urbanus's Tulou Collective Housing is a communal residence that integrates living, shopping, religion, and entertainment into one single building entity.

2017, while the average income per capita increased 2.5 times. National policy priorities shifted to address housing affordability issues. With elaborate market regulations and affordable housing initiatives on the way, a transition to a public-private mixed-ownership housing system was on the horizon. →

→ Lying along the central axis of Beijing, Dashilan is around 1.8 miles (3 kilometers) south of the Forbidden City. Connecting the main streets of Dashilan are narrow alleys called *hutong*, where residential units in the form of courtyard houses are located. These single-story dwellings, or *siheyuan*, are common throughout northern China. They are usually built around a quadrangle and arranged in accordance with Confucian familial

↑ The Shangwei Village Plug-In Houses by People's Architecture Office are renovated houses that are hundreds of years old.

→ MAD's proposal for the "Future of Hutongs" features metallic bubbles scattered over Beijing's oldest neighborhoods.

principles and traditional feng-shui. For example, the entrance gate is often on the southern side, and the revered elder members of the family live in the northern rooms facing the gate.

Before the socialist republic was established in 1949, China's living space per capita was only around 32 square feet (three square meters). In the early years of socialist transformation, privately owned houses in major cities like Beijing were bought or confiscated by the state. Under the newly established socialist regime, it was common to split or segment courtyard houses, originally intended for a single extended family, and divide them between several smaller households. These traditional courtyard houses often lack modern amenities and they can be difficult to modify because of the fragility of their structures and increasingly strict building codes. In coastal cities like Shanghai or Guangzhou, old colonial or eclectic-style residential buildings were subject to similar redistribution processes in the socialist era, resulting in comparable problems today. In this context, innovative *hutong* renewal solutions may serve as models for the revival of old towns in other regions.

While PAO's courtyard renovation of a *siheyuan* focuses on adding functionality and space in an affordable manner, other architects have focused on different aspects of *hutongs*'

potential. Zhang Ke and his practice ZAO/standardarchitecture created a 323-square-foot (30-square-meter) hostel with five guest rooms as part of their Micro Hutong Renewal project while Ma Yansong and MAD Architects imagined metallic bubbles scattered throughout Beijing's oldest neighborhoods. These projects pay homage to traditional Chinese ways of life and strive to retain traditional values while giving residents the benefits of modern lifestyles.

As China moves towards a mixed-ownership system, affordable and social housing will play a bigger role in the country's housing provision, and therefore, public housing is set to become a new testing ground for architectural innovation—creating a rare opportunity for Chinese architects to pursue social

This plug-in structure by People's Architecture Office can be assembled by a few people in one day, requiring no special skills.

The prefabricated panels are light, easy to handle, and inexpensive to ship.

change through design. Urbanus's Tulou Collective Housing, built in Guangdong in 2008, is one such experimental public housing project. Taking inspiration from *tulou*, the traditional ring-shaped communal residences unique to the region's Hakka people, the structure integrates living spaces, storage, commerce, ritual, and public entertainment. Subsidies provided by the government reduce the cost of units, making →

These projects pay homage to traditional Chinese ways of life and strive to retain traditional values while giving residents the benefits of modern lifestyles.

Public housing is set to become a new testing ground for architectural innovation—creating a rare opportunity for Chinese architects to pursue social change through design.

As China moves toward a mixed-ownership system, social housing will play a bigger role.

→ this audacious, affordable housing experiment viable. While Urbanus introduced the traditional Hakka lifestyle into the contemporary urban fabric, Atelier GOM's Longnan Garden Social Housing Estate focuses on the benefits of outdoor spaces for residents, and the flower-filled housing complex in Shanghai proves that public housing can be both aesthetically pleasing and conceptually cutting-edge.

In southern China, the process of urbanization took a more dazzling and less regulated route. The speed of change is most apparent in the Pearl River Delta (PRD), a densely populated lowland region that encompasses nine major cities, including Guangzhou and Shenzhen. Since the reform and opening-up of China in 1978, the area has undergone rapid modernization, and according to a World Bank report it became the world's largest megalopolis in both size and population in 2015. PRD's phenomenal development and economic growth lifted millions of people out of poverty.

Shenzhen, the rock star within PRD, started its wild journey when it was designated a Special Economic Zone (SEZ) in 1980. From 1990 to 2010, Shenzhen's GDP grew more than 50 times. Today, it is a global innovation hub, often referred to as the Silicon Valley of China.

The myth that Shenzhen was only a "small fishing village" when designated SEZ and grew to a megacity in 30 years has been circulating for years, but it is a reductive rags-to-riches narrative that ignores the region's original inhabitants and histories. A phenomenon common to PRD and many other major Chinese cities is the so-called "urban village." A result of poor planning decisions or policies, urban villages are formed when cities expand around preexisting villages. They are commonly found in city outskirts, but sometimes they form the downtown areas of major cities and tend to be inhabited by impoverished populations, but they also offer low-cost accommodation to migrants arriving in the area.

PAO's project in Shenzhen tackles the housing problems associated with urban villages directly. Their Shangwei Village Plug-In House is an iteration of their signature paneled houses that appear as though they are literally plugged into the surrounding context. The rampant urbanization of Shenzhen engulfed several villages, including Shangwei, where the migration of the village population had left many properties abandoned and in poor condition. The village government collaborated with PAO to regenerate the village and create new spaces for artists and artisans from greater Shenzhen. The Village Plug-In House project involves building new structures inside the existing houses with a modular approach that preserves the existing fabric of the buildings. In the context of China's ongoing urbanization, the intelligent approach of PAO's utilitarian and inexpensive plug-in houses is much needed.

Though not immediately scalable due to their site-specific nature, the projects of Urbanus, People's Architecture Office, and other forward-thinking Chinese architects, excel because they recognize residents' agency in the urban renewal process. The future of housing in China lies in this generative and empowering approach to urban renewal, and the creative and visionary reconciliation between the old and the new. ▮

Atelier GOM's Longnan Garden Social Housing Estate proves that public housing can be aesthetically pleasing.

The Plug-In House leaves the original structure untouched while a new structure is built inside the existing house.

The smarter future of housing in China contrasts with the usual "demolish and rebuild" model, which has been the driving force of China's urbanization for decades.

DESIGNER	J. C. Architecture
PROJECT	JCA Living Lab
LOCATION	Taipei, Taiwan

Old Vibes, New Energy: Adapting Historical Spaces to Suit a Modern Lifestyle

J.C. Architecture found a number of innovative ways to breathe new life into the disparate spaces of this early 20th-century, inner-city Taipei residence, which includes university dormitory rooms that were added in the 1950s. The design of the single-story abode, refurbished with a young family in mind, prioritizes the connection between the inside and outside spaces—each room has its own function, but also serves as an area to pass through as you move from one activity to the next. The main bathroom links to the living room, the backyard, and the kitchen-dining area, for example. Overhead, generous skylights allow sunlight to flood the spaces below, while offering welcome glimpses of sky and the verdant garden outside. A wall separates the most private rooms of the house—which also happen to be the oldest—from the more open, public spaces, allowing the architects to maintain a deliberate contrast between the historical and the contemporary elements of their scheme. Old brick walls, wooden-beamed ceilings, and opaque Japanese-style screens are juxtaposed with concrete finishes, wire-mesh structures, and ceramic tiling, and between the two halves, a bright-red front door symbolizes the infusion of new energy into the old. At the rear of the house, a red ladder rises up above the lush planting to the roof, connecting the home to the ground and the sky. ▌

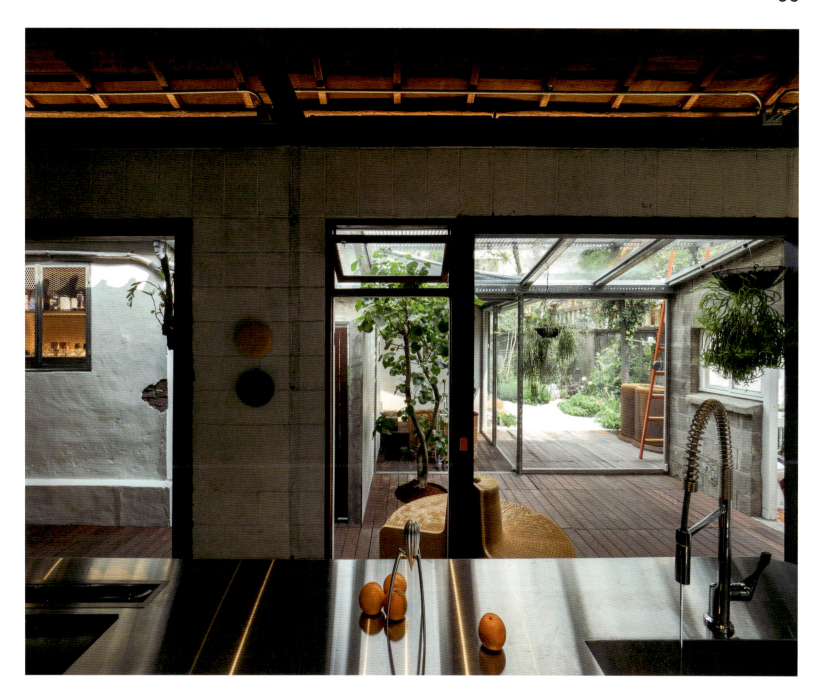

↑ Seen beyond the kitchen here, the garden is an
    important element in the refurbishment, forging
    a strong connection with nature.

← Rooms include spaces in which children can play.
    Here, a roll of brown paper makes for a great
    opportunity to paint, draw, and color on a big scale.

↑　Floor-to-ceiling windows overlooking the garden help
　　to extend the house, toward the outdoors.

←　Rough, whitewashed walls and crazy paving offer
　　a neutral backdrop for furnishings of all kinds—a nod
　　to the architects' desire that the spaces should evolve
　　with their inhabitants.

↓　Minimal, freestanding furnishings allow rooms to remain
　　flexible, their uses to be determined as the family grows.

This Piece of "Architectural Furniture" Compartmentalizes a Room for a Range of Domestic Activities

This room with a tall, sweeping, semicircular window overlooking the garden, in a large 1930s house located in what was once the salubrious French Concession district of Shanghai has seen many permutations, from the ballroom of a bourgeois family home to the whole abode for a family sharing communal amenities with others. Following a renovation at the hands of architects Atelier tao+c, it now serves as a compact contemporary living space for a single occupant, or two at most, thanks to an innovative piece of micro "furniturization" architecture. The free-standing geometric volume occupies the back of the room, leaving the original walls, windows, and ceiling intact. Made from maple plywood, it compartmentalizes the space into a series of living areas and activity spaces—shower, kitchen, dining room, and living room. The densely layered composition also includes a series of niches, cupboards, and bookshelves for discrete storage. The second level, on top of the structure, accommodates modest sleeping and study areas. A wooden staircase leads from the living room to the bedroom, and a thin metal ladder connects the study area with the dining space. There are no physical partitions in the room, making it feel light and spacious, and the structure makes maximum use of the available space, facilitating all of the essential functions of day-to-day living. ▌

DESIGNER	Atelier tao+c
PROJECT	U-Shaped Room
LOCATION	Shanghai

↑ Sight lines to all corners of this dwelling reveal how compact it is at a single glance.

← Sinking the kitchen to a lower level and defining the space with red brick tiles helps give the room fluidity.

→ The design packs in a phenomenal amount of storage space.

DESIGNER	TAOA
PROJECT	Two-Fold Yard
LOCATION	Beijing

Beneath This Beijing Home Lies a Subterranean Studio Space for Artistic Endeavors

This refurbished three-story Beijing home owned by a celebrated artist and his family is a work of stark contrasts. It centers on what Beijing-based architects TAOA call its "two-fold yard." The yard marks the division between two contrasting spaces within the dwelling, each with a distinct function, character, and atmosphere. It is two-fold because it functions as the studio's roof while also providing the family with a beautifully planted terrace. Above ground, there is a series of warm, bright, rooms where the family lives, and below, a cool working space that serves as a studio, allowing the artist to work uninterrupted. The two areas exist as completely separate, albeit parallel, entities; while the space above ground is wrapped in warm wood and translucent perforated aluminum panels, the underground studio space is lined with bare concrete. And where natural light floods into the domestic rooms surrounding the open courtyard, the workspace below is illuminated by shafts of light that enter via subterranean courtyards at each end of the structure, meaning that the space shifts markedly from light to dark and back to light again. And while the living space on the upper level is filled with sights and sounds from outside, the studio is quiet and still—the perfect ambiance for independent thought and creative work. ▮

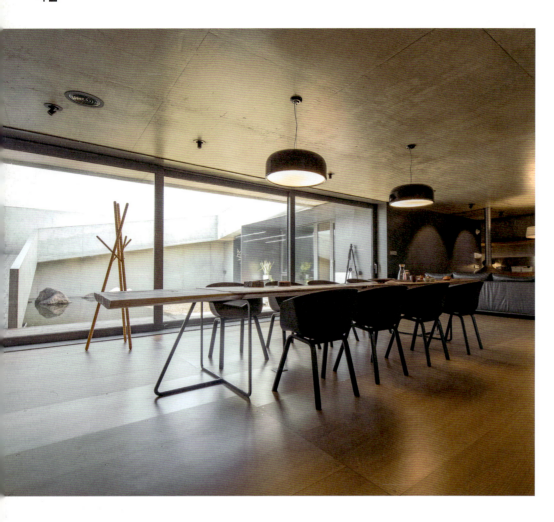

↑ The subterranean art studio is an open-plan flexible space in which the artist can work and meet with associates—close by his family, but without interruption.

→ The beautifully planted upper courtyard is flanked with generous timber decking.

↓ Beyond the artist's studio, a sloping, timber-decked path winds around a pond-filled courtyard and up to the level above.

DESIGNER	Zhaoyang Architects
PROJECT	Zhu'an Residence
LOCATION	Xizhou, Dali, Yunnan Province

A Patchwork of Rooms Interlocks with Covered Walkways and Verdant Courtyards in This Artist's Residence

In their design for the home of Chinese painter Zhong Meng and his wife, Zhaoyang Architects exploited the inward-looking characteristic of the traditional courtyard house to create a home where inside and outside spaces have equal footing. The house is located on the eastern edge of Chengbei Village in Xizhou Town, Dali. It is close to the village amenities and also benefits from a semi-rural position overlooking open fields. In order to maximize views of the outside space, the architects stitched the functional areas together with a series of nine courtyards of various sizes, meaning that every room of the abode has a leafy outlook, and everyday life is completely integrated with the enjoyment of the continuous garden. A path leads from the street entrance to a southern courtyard from which a long corridor offers quick access to the private quarters, themselves connected to four further courtyards of various sizes and functions that bring abundant natural light and ventilation to the interiors. On one side of the living room, a large aperture overlooks a pond in the central courtyard, while another looks out across green fields. In keeping with the vernacular architecture, the facades of the house are rendered in lime plaster mixed with straw. Simply detailed and rigidly geometric, they allow the eye to linger instead on the beauty within—the lush vegetation of the courtyards and the painter's collections of furniture and antiques. ∎

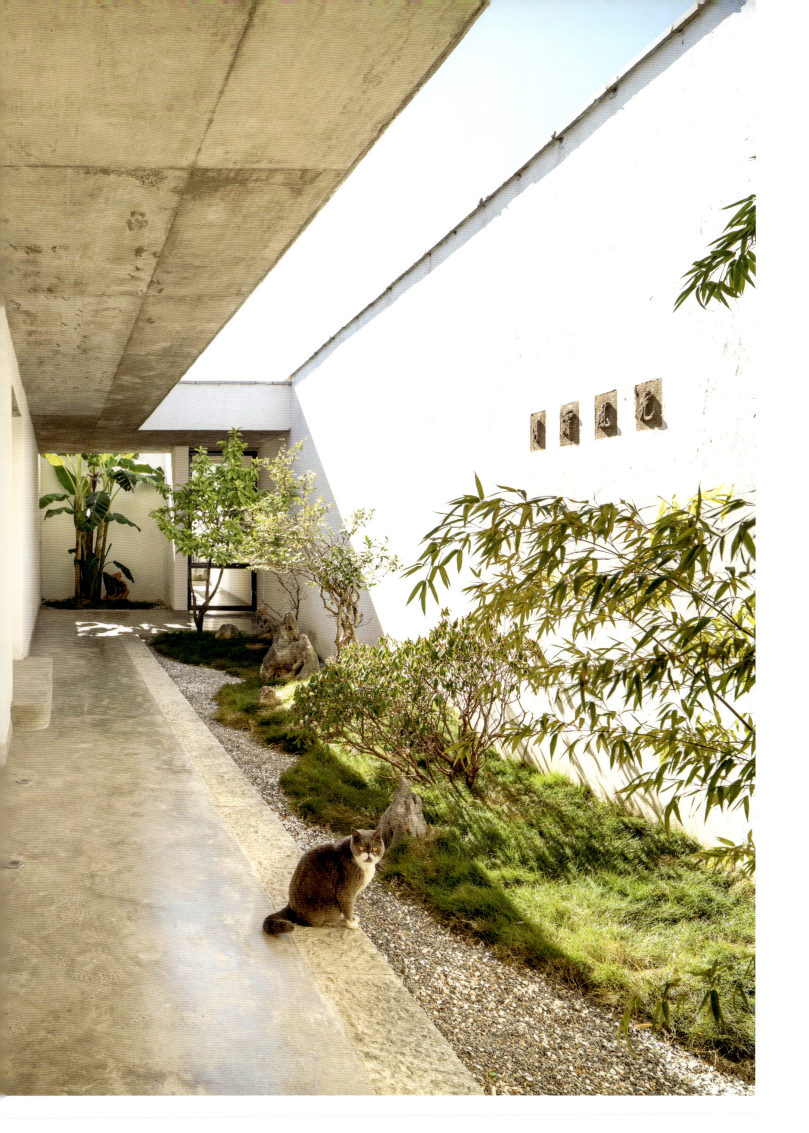

→ Floor-to-ceiling windows keep the internal spaces light, despite large roof overhangs.

↘ Inside the house, interior features are kept to a minimum so that it's the furnishings themselves that shine.

↓ Slab roofs and partition walls segment the external space into a series of outdoor "rooms."

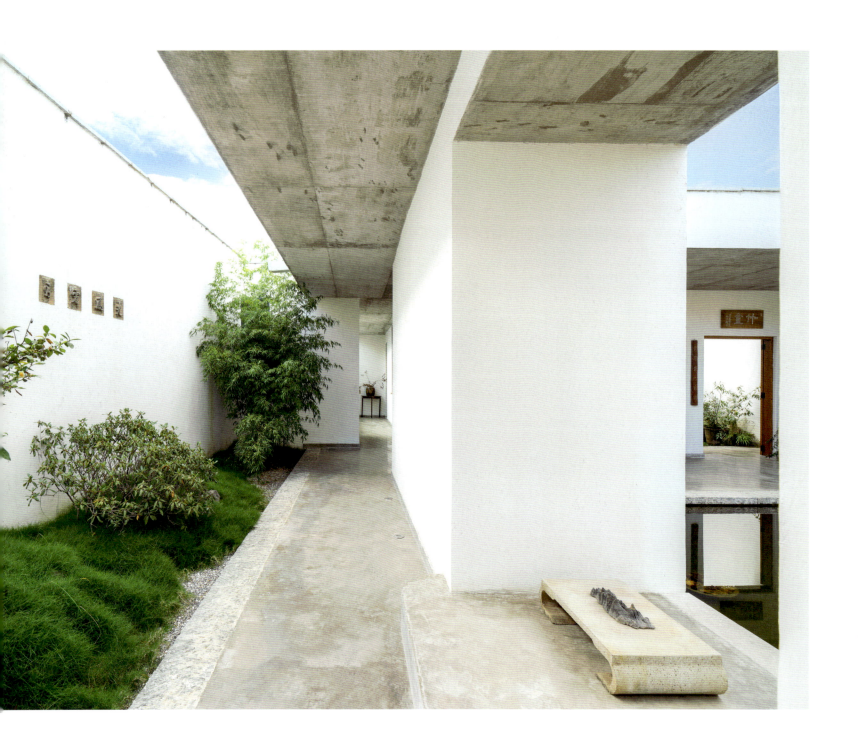

DESIGNER	Zhaoyang Architects
PROJECT	Sunyata Hotel
LOCATION	Dali, Yunnan Province

A Collection of Traditional Dwellings Unfolds to Reveal a State-of-the-Art Hotel Complex

Facing challenges at almost every stage, Zhaoyang Architects applied a good deal of lateral thinking in their scheme for this 14-room boutique hotel in the heart of Dali old town, Yunnan Province. With the site surrounded on three sides by residential buildings, the immediate challenge was that the hotel did not offer any views overlooking the city. The solution was to build the hotel in such a way that all of the rooms were oriented toward a small but serene courtyard space at the center of the building. Flanking the courtyard to the east—the only side of the building open to the street—is a transparent space housing a cafe. Passersby can see right through the space and into the courtyard beyond. The rest of the building comprises eight separate volumes, arranged in various ways so that the size, interior arrangement, and the position of each hotel room's openings are unique. A further challenge for the architects was that, in order to remain unobtrusive in its old-town setting, the hotel had to have a traditional facade facing the street, and 80 percent of its roof had to be covered in traditional tiles. So, while the concrete facades overlooking the courtyard are resolutely modern, the street facade is rendered in stone, and seven of the eight volumes are topped with double-pitched tiled roofs. The effect creates a sense of amazement on arrival because visitors progress from what appears to be a traditional old-town building at street level to the minimalist haven beyond. ▌

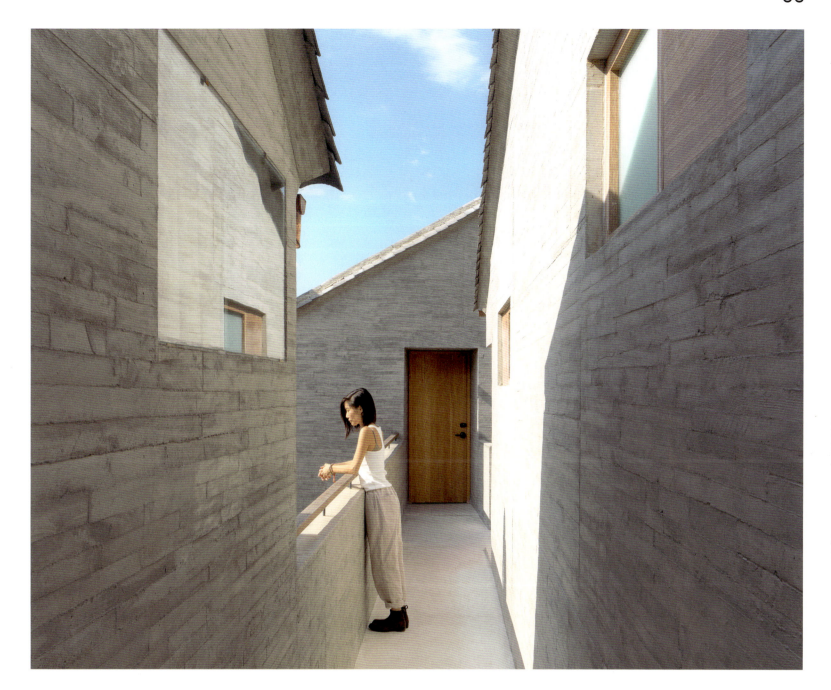

↑ Traditional tiles and contemporary concrete surfaces create an intriguing play between village vernacular and modernity.

← The uniformity of the concrete structures with their timber-framed windows and doors conjures an almost village-like atmosphere.

↑   Looking down the length of the tea room and
into the lush courtyard beyond.

→   Each of the apartments in the hotel is different
in its design, offering a multitude of different
experiences to be had.

DESIGNER	DAS Lab
PROJECT	Lost Villa Boutique Hotel
LOCATION	Zhongwei, Ningxia Province

A Village-Like Desert Hotel Stands in the Shadow of the Great Wall

Close to the banks of the Yellow River and with views of the Great Wall of China in the distance, this fifteen-room hotel blends seamlessly into the desert landscape. Inspired by the vernacular architecture, Lost Villa Boutique Hotel in Zhongwei, Ningxia Province, is a short distance from the one-time frontier city now known as Dawan Village. Designed by Shanghai-based architects DAS Lab, it features a series of organically arranged low-rise, flat-roofed volumes interspersed with terraces, wooden walkways, and gravel courtyards. Reed canopies shade the outside spaces from the intense sunlight and cast an intriguing pattern of stripes on the facades beneath. A specially developed mortar covers both the interior and exterior walls to emulate the rustic texture of the rammed-earth dwellings typical in the local area, and in time, exposure to the seasonal winds and rains will give them the same worn patina. Inside, DAS Lab deliberately styled each room differently, experimenting with different models, scales, and materials to reconfigure the relationship between the room's occupants and the natural environment surrounding the hotel. The windows frame views across the landscape toward the river or the forest of fruit trees nearby, and all of the rooms share the same palette of neutral stone and slate gray with clean lines and natural wood furnishings. Light plays an important role—the bedrooms are predominantly dark with narrow openings in the facade that channel shafts of light across the walls and floors and ceilings, while the living rooms are bright and airy with larger apertures. ▍

↑   Framing pockets of vegetation intensifies their impact, making visitors more aware of the natural surroundings.

→   There is a constant play of light and shade across the textured walls of the buildings.

←   The desert is a place of extremes—hot summers and punishingly cold winters. Many of the buildings have limited windows to help control temperatures within.

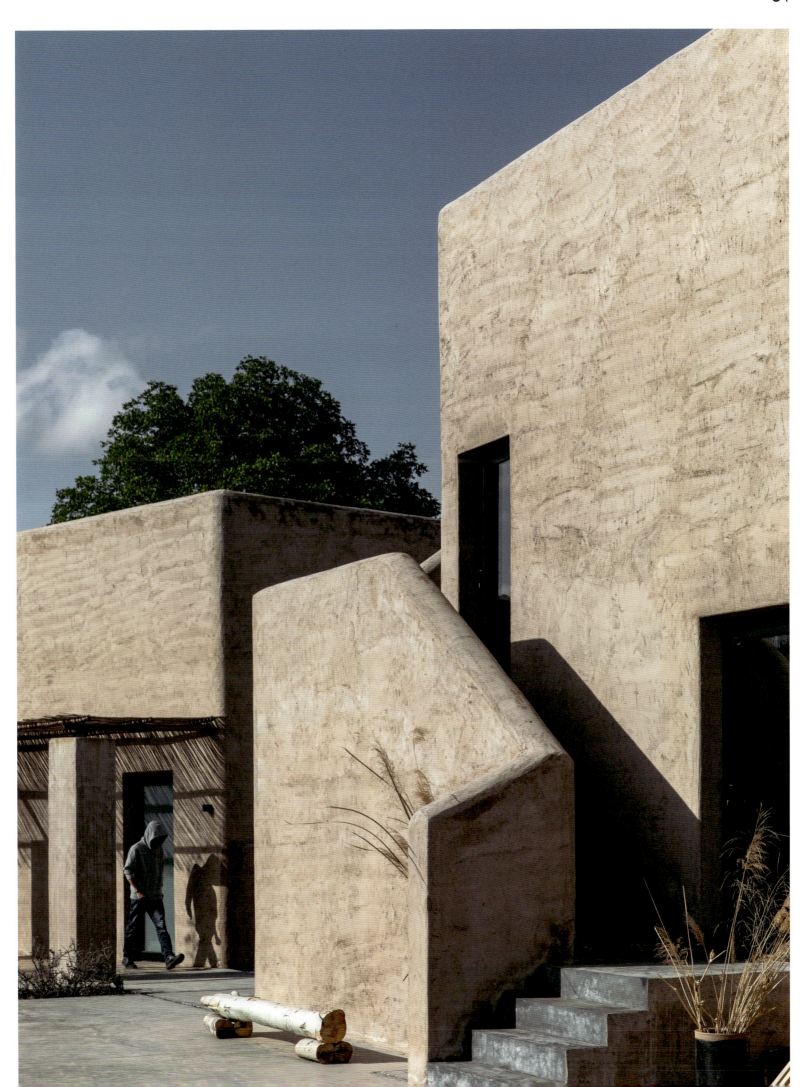

↑ The earthy tones of the hotel's facades enable the
hotel to nestle comfortably into the desert landscape.

← The multiple terraces, courtyards, and rooftop galleries
encourage hotel guests to spend more time outdoors.

← With their reeded canopies and wood-strip
flooring, the external corridors offer inside-outside
space that blurs the boundaries.

↙ Each of the rooms at the hotel overlooks a small,
walled garden space with outdoor seating.

↓ Inside the hotel, the cool, shaded rooms have
wood finishes and cement walls to match those
of the exterior.

DESIGNER	hyperSity Architects
PROJECT	Cave House in Loess Plateau
LOCATION	Weinan

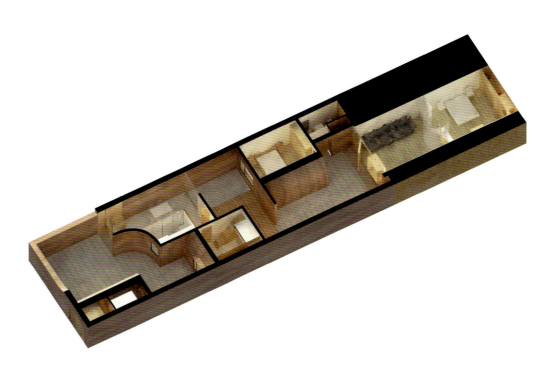

The Timely Contemporary Makeover of a Timeless Subterranean Home

The *yaodong*, is an ancient Chinese courtyard cave-dwelling that is particularly associated with the Loess Plateau in northern China. Typically dug into the earth, the rooms are well insulated in winter and refreshingly cool in summer, making them extremely energy efficient. This contemporary refurbishment of a *yaodong* in Weinan, Shaanxi Province, by hyperSity Architects, suggests that the form could continue to serve as a staple of the 21st century and beyond. The architects decided to preserve the main room at the rear of the original development and start again with the three subsidiary rooms in the courtyard. This allowed them to maximize the geothermal properties of the building while increasing the natural light and ventilation available throughout. Two structures bring additional light into the main room, now arranged as two rooms—a bedroom and a living room. The first is a glass column between the two rooms, which functions as a light well. The second is the open wood-and-glass lattice wall at the end of the living room. Five further volumes arranged in a dynamic layout around the courtyard provide a second bedroom, a dining room, a kitchen, a bathroom, and storage space, and a path zigzags from one room to the next. Despite the contemporary design, the building remains rooted in tradition—the footprint and overall height of the home are unchanged, and the new walls were built using vernacular rammed-earth construction methods. ▌

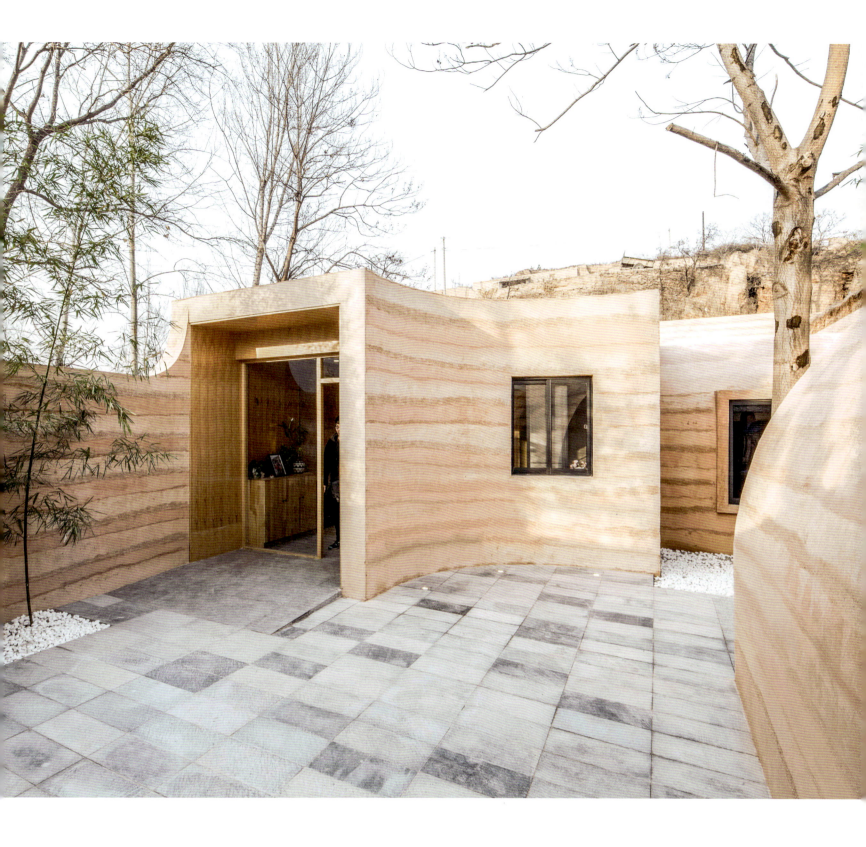

↑ Inside the newly landscaped front yard, looking toward the entrance to the dining room/kitchen area.

← The unique texture and color of the rammed-earth walls comes from the local clay.

→ A skywell brings natural light into the rooms at the center of the house.

↘ Throughout the design, the strength of the rammed-earth walls is countered by the warmth and simplicity of wood finishes.

↓ The dining room/kitchen area benefits from a courtyard at each end, to allow for maximum light and ventilation.

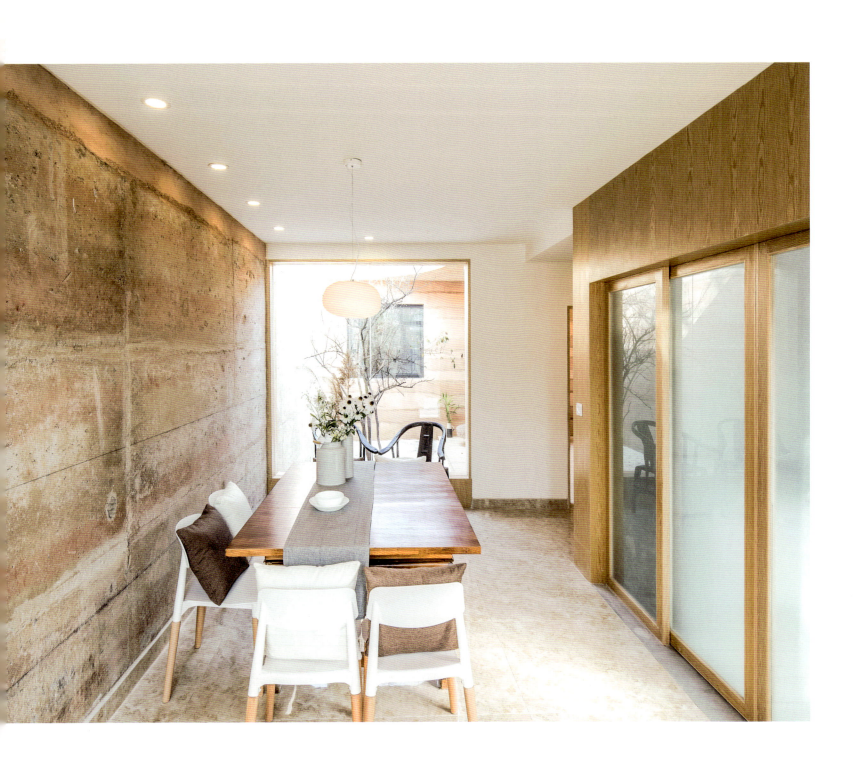

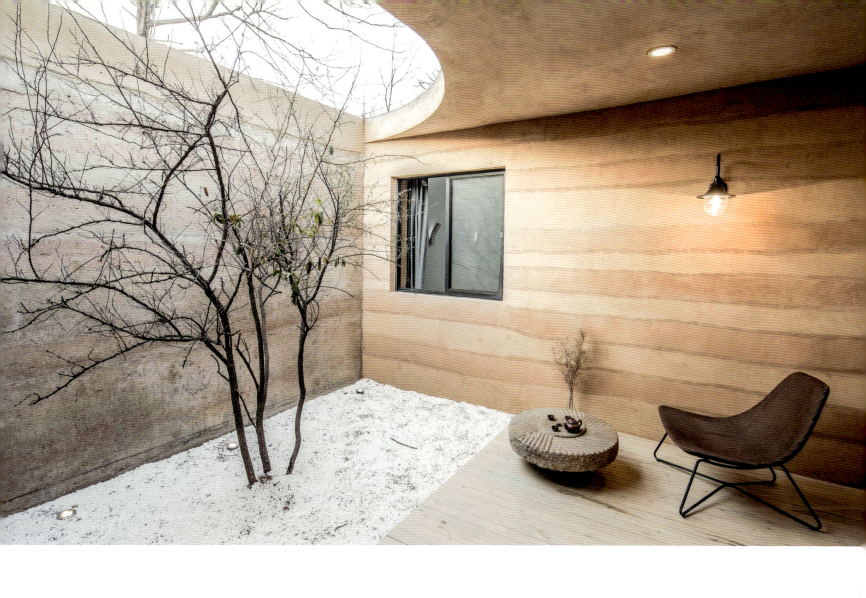

↑   The main entrance to the original cave dwelling
    has a curtain wall of wood and glass to allow light
    into the rooms beyond.

←   Plants inside and out help to maintain a tranquil
    atmosphere.

DESIGNER	Design Institute of Landscape and Architecture China Academy of Art
PROJECT	Boat Rooms on the Fuchun River
LOCATION	Meicheng, Jiande

Lakeside Hotel Rooms Offer the Ultimate in Romance, Peace, and Tranquility

Not far from the city of Jiande and around 3 miles (5 kilometers) east of the ancient town of Meicheng in China's southern region of Changjiang, the tranquil Yanzhu Lake forms where a natural spring from Wulong Mountain flows into the Fuchun River. The surface of the lake is completely still, and a series of wooden arches are reflected at the water's edge. The arches are, in fact, the prows of five boat rooms that belong to the Fuchun New Century Wonderland Resort. The rooms created by the Design Institute of Landscape and Architecture China Academy of Art take inspiration from the unique boat-living culture of the fishing families who lived here in the Ming and middle Qing dynasties. Nestled among the trees, the stern of each "boat" rests on the riverbank, while the prow is raised on stilts firmly planted in the lake's bed, its soaring glass facade maximizing the expansive views of the misty waters that lie beyond. Constructed almost entirely from wood—red cedar, Douglas fir, and gingko—the boat rooms echo the form and structure of traditional vessels. On arrival, guests enter at the stern, which also houses the bathroom. An open-plan living space unfolds before culminating in an oversized balcony that stretches out above the surface of the lake. In the middle of the room, above the bed, a skylight allows guests to enjoy sunlight and shadows cast by the trees during the day, and the star-filled sky at night. ▌

↑   The resort takes on an atmospheric air come twilight
    as the warm glow of the boat room lights is reflected
    in the still water.

→   The boat room's structural frame comprises a series
    of arch girders and log beams and is clearly visible
    from both inside and out.

WUTOPIA LAB

Nearly two decades in the gray world of large-scale architecture propelled studio founders Yu Ting and Min Erni to develop an unconventional style that fuses complexity, artifice, and a bit of magic.

Yu Ting and Min Erni, the husband-and-wife duo who founded Wutopia Lab in 2013, might be considered relatively new to the game, in architecture terms at least, but, in fact, quite the opposite is true. Before establishing Wutopia Lab, Yu had risen through the ranks to become deputy chief architect at the large state-owned company he had joined in 1995. When Yu left the company, his departure was an incalculably important one, although he describes it in a characteristically prosaic manner: "I felt a bit bored [at the previous job], and I wanted to experiment with design, so we founded Wutopia Lab." Seven years later, the duo's desire for continual experimentation and specifically to examine the highly experiential capacity of architecture is something that can be seen throughout the Shanghai-based studio's projects.

Nowhere is this more clearly expressed than at the Eight Tenths Garden completed in 2017. A truly mixed-use development occupying only around 21,530 square feet (2,000 square meters), the architects describe the project as a "micro cultural complex." This one-of-a-kind building performs a surprising number of functions, including a museum of enamel manufacturing, a garden open to the public, coffee shop, restaurant, bed-and-breakfast accommodation, and the office for a modern enamel design brand. All of this is housed in a renovated four-story cylindrical structure with a two-story former sales office underneath.

Wutopia Lab has stated its desire to reject "obsessive minimalism" while avoiding "exaggerated scenes" lacking spatial connection, consciously reinforcing a sense of contradiction. At the Eight Tenths Garden, the result is a purposeful juxtaposition that the architects have called "using antithesis to unfold the space." The complex exterior facade contrasts with the harmonious atmosphere of the interior →

Wutopia Lab has stated its desire to reject "obsessive minimalism" while avoiding "exaggerated scenes" lacking spatial connection, consciously reinforcing a sense of contradiction.

← Eight Tenths Garden in Shanghai. Its skin becomes transparent as dusk descends on the city.

↑ In the enamel museum, a "keyhole" opening looks out into the garden.

← Each of the bed-and-breakfast suites has access to its own courtyard space.

↙ The uppermost structure of the building has a roof of traditional gray tiles around a central courtyard, accessible to all B & B guests.

↓ The two buildings surrounding the garden at ground level are clad in a black grille curtain wall, creating a calm, unified backdrop for this tranquil setting.

→ spaces. The cylindrical structure, surrounded by an almost kitsch, 1970s-inspired rock garden, is wrapped with perforated white aluminum screens, folded to resemble the pleats of a fan. The screens diffuse the sunlight as it enters the building and mediate lines of sight between the internal and external environments. Clever interlacing of gardens and interior spaces has delivered a much-loved community asset. The enormously varied spaces inside and out "reveal the spirit of Shanghai," according to Wutopia Lab—an urban life with an innate richness, restrained, and yet welcoming.

In the heart of the ancient city of Yangzhou, Wutopia Lab's multilayered approach is further intensified at the Slow Yangzhou×Xinhua Bookstore, which was completed in 2019. With a mission to facilitate what the architects consider the past, present, and future of Yangzhou, the project represents a tireless effort to contrive a spatial adventure. A series of multifunctional spaces accommodate a bookstore, hostel, an exhibition space, conference facilities, and a tea house. A succession of "boxes" offer radically different interior and exterior experiences for the visitor: the brightly lit Weightless Box makes a drastic departure from the dark gray of the dense urban fabric outside, and then a Jewelry Box (for children), Nature Box, and Surprise Box, which includes a series of three secrets to be discovered by visitors.

Some of the spaces designed by Wutopia Lab are labyrinthine in nature, and some might consider them over-labored. But Yu is quick to refute the notion that any of the studio's projects are solely ornamental or non-functional: "I don't regard my design as decorative," he says resolutely. "The decorative is more focused on surface, while we are interested in creating space." He likes to go back to the notion of contrasts, with elements →

↑ Slow Yangzhou×Xinhua Bookstore. In the bright, light Weightless Box, bookshelves made of white acrylic create a visual effect of fog and a sense of floating.

→ The bookstore courtyard is left empty deliberately—the antithesis of the busy city street beyond. A lone red maple tree is its only feature.

← Plain House. In this renovation for Chinese artist Li Bin, Wutopia Lab painted the vast living room in Li Bin's trademark red.

↑ All other walls of the house—inside and out—remain a uniform gray.

↓ Inside, the radiance of the red changes owing to a singular skylight positioned in the southwest corner of the living room ceiling.

Yu Ting has an almost child-like explanation for his fixation: "Daily life is not always good or exciting, so I want to create spaces that are unfamiliar, that you have the motivation to come and see."

→ of his projects representing complexity and others showing an urge for simplicity. One project that shows Wutopia Lab's capacity for a more stripped-back lucidity is Paper House, at the Sun Commune in Linan. Here Yu went back to the very basics of traditional architecture, employing local artisans adept at the structural use of bamboo to create something that is astonishingly simple. With a creative impulse that swings between simplicity and complexity, it is intriguing to discover what the studio's design process entails. Yu points to an exhaustive journey of talking to the client at length for every project. Looking back to the Eight Tenths Garden, he is particularly proud of his ability to "persuade the client to create a museum," again showing Yu's natural aversion to anything that might be deemed straightforward.

Yu's own transition from the world of big architecture to something so thoroughly eclectic and frequently enchanting is plain. Perhaps this ultimate contrast in the way architecture is practiced is the greatest influence on Wutopia Lab. Yu often alludes to what he calls magical realism as a source of inspiration. He has an almost child-like explanation for this fixation: "Daily life is not always good or exciting, so I want to create spaces that are unfamiliar, that you have the motivation to come and see." With a diverse portfolio of generally small and intensely designed spaces, Wutopia is set to continue to attract attention and bewilderment in equal measure. ▌

← Wutopia Lab's Paper House for the Sun Commune, Linan, took inspiration from sketches of temporary teahouses in the works of ancient Chinese scholars.

↙ Local handmade oiled paper was chosen for its properties for creating silhouettes.

↓ Constructed in just seven days, the house was placed overlooking a reservoir in the commune.

DESIGNER	Studio 10
PROJECT	The Other Place
LOCATION	Guilin

Bringing M. C. Escher's Mysterious, Infinite, and Impossible Spaces to Life

As its name suggests, the Other Place, a guesthouse by the Li River in Pingle County, Guilin, conjures a fantastical realm of mystery, illusion, and whimsy. Guests must be prepared to suspend reality during their stay. Tasked with the brief of designing something "fresh, creative, unique, and otherworldly," Shenzhen-based architects Studio 10 sought inspiration from the works of graphic artist M.C. Escher for the styling of two suites here: Maze and Dream. Taking common motifs from Escher's "impossible" spaces, the architects filled the rooms—with ceilings as high as 23 feet (7 meters) in places—with staircases and secret doorways. Featuring a combination of two- and three-dimensional elements, some of which are functional, and others not, the interiors are dizzying, in terms of scale, proportion, and orientation. A somewhat synthetic color palette adds to the design's surreal nature: cotton-candy pink and white for one suite, and forest-green and gold for the other. There is something else uncanny about the rooms, something that takes a moment or two to sink in: all of the surfaces—floors, walls, ceilings, cupboards, and textiles are devoid of pattern, texture, fixtures, and fittings. The architects have taken great pains to keep any "real" components—lighting fixtures, electrical appliances—hidden within the structural fabric. The result is a series of pristine, fantastical rooms that fulfill the studio's desire to "differentiate the space from those we encounter in everyday life." ▐

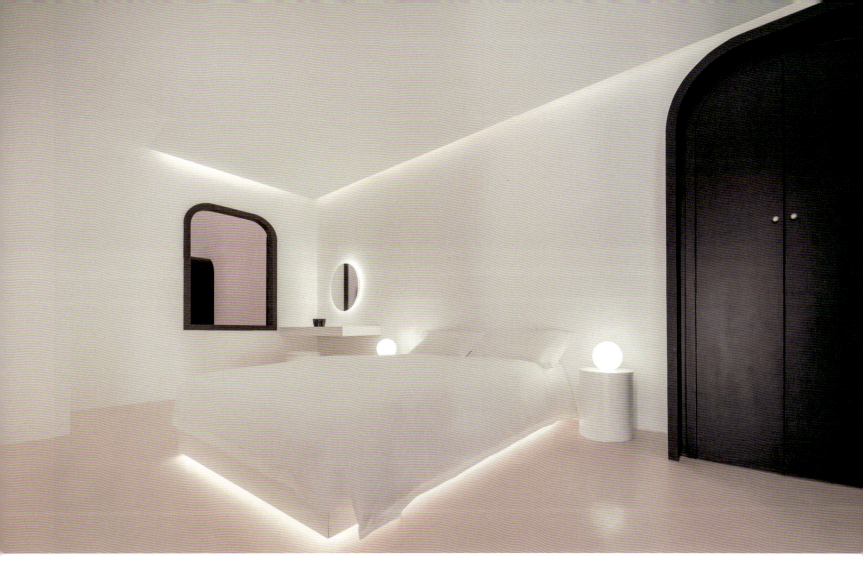

↑   In the words of the architect, the pink palette conjures an atmosphere that is "far from the chaos of mundane daily life."

←   The architect worked hard to balance Escher's mind-bending vision with the practical needs of the rooms.

→   In the green-themed room, "anti-gravitational" stairs lead to a mysterious golden door.

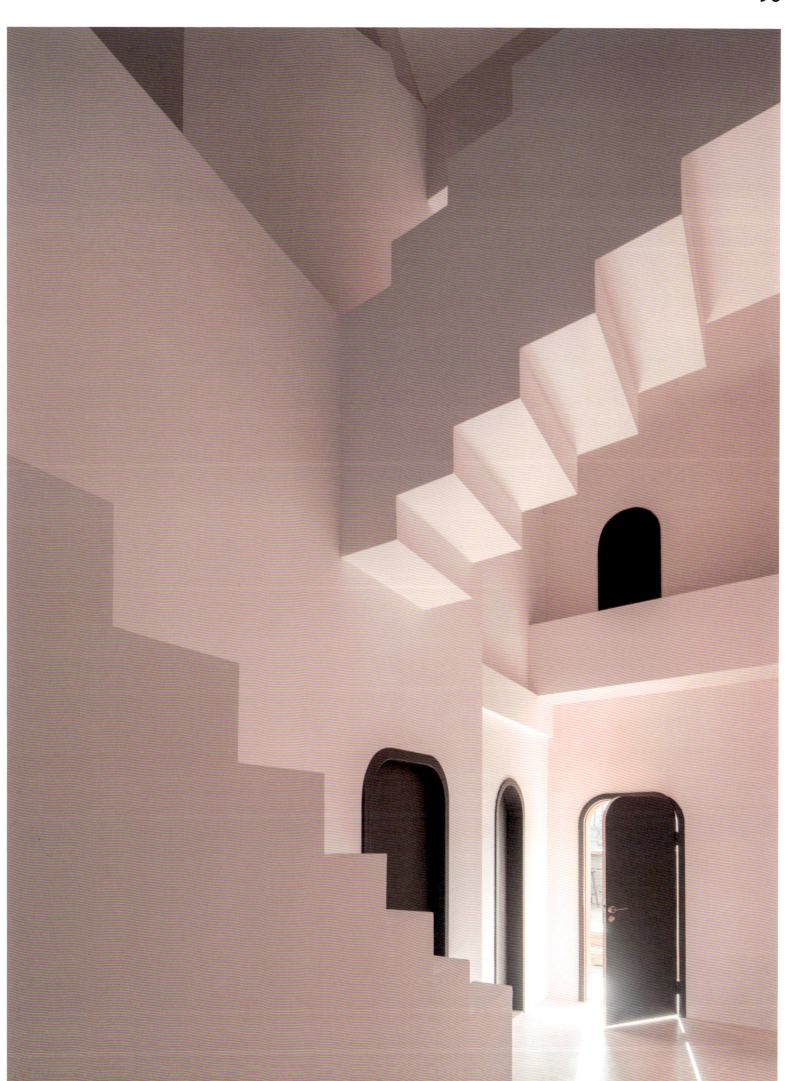

X+LIVING

Despite the pleasure-seeking spaces, it's not all fun and games for this successful Shanghai studio, although the founder clearly has business acumen when it comes to enjoyment.

"Playful" is used so often to describe the more exuberant works of architects and designers that the word is in very serious danger of losing its significance. With that in mind, referring to the prolific portfolio of Shanghai-based studio X+Living, which includes giant pastel flowers and M.C. Escher-like staircases, the word "playful" is somewhat redundant. And although this interior architecture practice's founder and director Li Xiang is known to enjoy watching her beloved cat attempting to type on her computer keyboard, and most of her projects have a fantasy-land quality, an air of complete professionalism abounds.

"Building a studio was not a sudden decision that flashed through my mind," says Li, looking back at life before she established the practice in 2011. She recalls that the projects she was working on at a government-run construction institute were based on conventional concepts and lacked creativity. Li was hankering for more innovation, and the chance to build something she felt was more connected to her values and spirit. "So I quit the job and founded my own studio," she says. X+Living has drawn much attention both at home and abroad thanks to what seems to be a shrewd commitment to the pursuit of architectural adventure and interior pleasure-seeking, and, it has to be said, for the exceptionally visual, photogenic quality of their output.

It is something of a paradox that the projects most demonstrably devoted to user experience, those that are built for children to play in, are X+Living's most articulate and arguably the most →

→ successful. Her extensive work for Neobio—a chain of indoor recreation centers for children and their parents—and, most notably, her designs for the center in Shenzhen show every bit of the dedication to spatial awareness and aesthetic consideration that the studio's founder is so keen to express. The miniature "cities," with numerous themed zones and fanciful parasols are all executed with rigor, rendering them far from frivolous from a design perspective. The tradition of architects designing spaces for children to play in has its roots in the modernist schemes of the 20th century and here in the shopping malls of 21st-century China. A continuation of the rationale developed during that period is evident in the studio's statements: "Division [of space] took into account the age groups, interests, and behaviors of kids, while at the same time combining functions for entertainment, education, and rest during parent-child activities." Photographs of the Neobio centers, devoid of children, give them a spooky, almost surreal quality akin to the much-fetishized image of the abandoned shopping mall. It is this uncanny quality that has made the projects a hit online.

At the Zhongshuge Bookstore in Chongqing, a mesmerizing hall lined with zigzag staircases that ascend and descend beside towering bookshelves creates a space reminiscent of an M.C. Escher print, which is maximized by a flawless mirrored ceiling. The configuration of the steps also recalls the ancient Chand Baori stepwell in Rajasthan, where a succession of steps draws the eye and, indeed, the body, deeper underground. On another floor, conical bookshelves interspersed with warmly lit reading nooks create a decidedly more welcoming environment for perusal. X+Living's creation at Chongqing appeared at the same time as several other voluminous explorations of the concept bookstore in China and East Asia at large; perhaps one of the more intriguing and certainly welcome developments →

← Shenzhen Neobio Family Park is home to the most fantastic miniature city, where kids can drive to bubble-shaped shops in toy cars along streets lined with towering parasols (previous pages).

→ At the Hangzhou Zhongshuge Bookstore, the children's reading room has shelves arranged around displays shaped like a train, a rollercoaster, and a pirate ship.

↘ In the "ladder hall" of the Chongqing Zhongshuge Bookstore, a mirrored ceiling only increases the dizzying, Escher-like disorientation sensation of the zigzagging staircases.

↓ The children's reading room of the Chongqing Zhongshuge Bookstore is lined with walls depicting Chongqing's landscape, buildings, and transportation.

"I see a wonderful and dreamy world, and I just want to show it to the public."
—Li Xiang

↑ The playful lobby of the New Century Magic Hotel in Huzhou.

→ All public spaces in this hotel are bright and colorful, with motifs harking back to art deco and Memphis Style.

→ of a flourishing, if sometimes exaggerated world of retail interiors. Li, however, still seems enthusiastic about the industry and insists that inspiration often comes from simple pleasures such as reading a book. "I see a wonderful and dreamy world, and I just want to show it to the public."

Of course, X+Living's output is far from restricted to concept bookstores and children's play centers; hotels, tea rooms, and other commercial spaces designed by the studio also exhibit the studio's signature bold and gregarious approach. The Park Zoo Hotel in Hangzhou and the New Century Magic Hotel in Huzhou show a generous desire to stimulate the guest (both child and adult), whether through an animal theme that combines figurative and abstract art or through a much-amplified rendition of the postmodernist Memphis style. In Chengdu, the restricted 1033-square-foot (96-square-meter) space occupied by the Zhuyeqing Green Tea Flagship Store, completed in 2019, also demonstrates X+Living's tireless pursuit of visual and experiential entertainment. "Drinking tea requires both a favorable environment and a good mood," states the project's literature, and, through a series of peculiar flying-saucer-like pods representing a "cloud and mountain" motif from freehand ink paintings, the designers have delivered this dutifully. With so many different styles, symbols, and inspirations, some might find it hard to trace the presence of a thread, or what might be called a "design philosophy" behind the studio's output, but Li insists that each of her projects "pursues the integration of spatial, artistic aesthetics with practical function," adding that "the styles can be changed, but the core principle is always upheld."

With an acumen for enjoyment, Li and the studio she founded is illustrating, with a colorful palette at her disposal, a flair for artistic expression in the most commercial of sectors. X+Living's director acknowledges a new zeitgeist in China today, something that she is no doubt part of. "Design has changed from uniform reproduction, which neglects both aesthetics and experience, to something more exquisite, abundant, full of personality and diversity." However, Li, ever tied to her desk, is the first to admit that it isn't all fun: "Of course, the process of creation is enjoyable, and I can't help myself," she says, "but self-initiated demands constantly accumulate pressure on me, and they are not released until the project is completed." It is a case of all work and plenty of play at this busy Shanghai office. ▮

Li Xiang insists that each of her projects "pursues the integration of spatial, artistic aesthetics with practical function; the styles can be changed, but the core principle is always upheld."

↑   The smooth, soft, sculptural form of X+Living's "clouds" and "mountains" at the Zhuyeqing Green Tea Flagship Store.

→   Some mountains serve as shelving for product display, while others function as pods with sofas for relaxing.

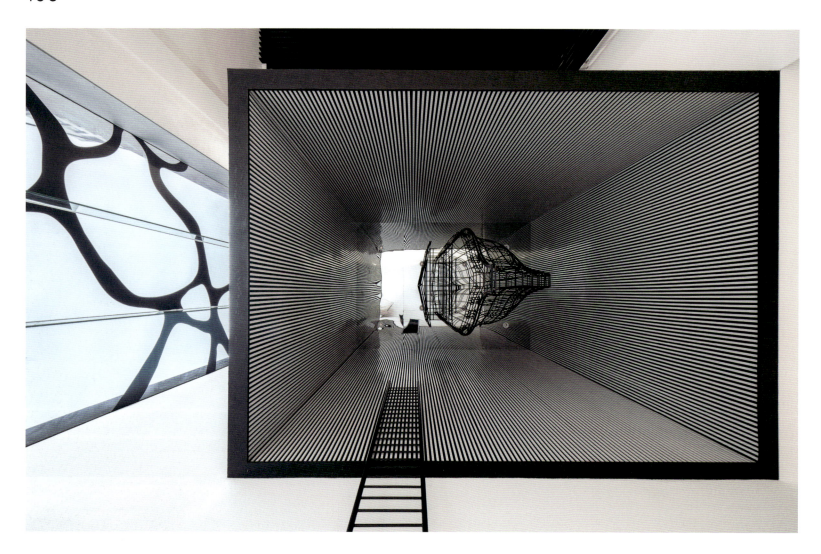

↑ At Park Zoo Hotel, X+Living have created art
installations that combine abstract pieces with
functional pieces that guests can use as furniture.

→ Part of the architect's desire for this scheme is to
provoke feelings of compassion for the world's
endangered animals.

Human Endeavor, Art, and Nature Converge in this Sublime Opera House

Rising from the wetlands surrounding Harbin's Songhua River in northern China, the Harbin Opera House is part of an extensive cultural center designed by MAD Architects, which includes a central public plaza, a recreation center, and a wetland park. At the heart of the concept lies the architects' desire to create, in the words of founding principal Ma Yansong, "a cultural center of the future—a tremendous performance venue, as well as a dramatic public space that embodies the integration of human, art, and the city identity, while synergistically blending with the surrounding nature." The focal highlight of the scheme, the opera house's sinuous form, lies low, sprawling across the natural landscape. The structure, built from white stone and concrete and clad in custom-made, pure-white aluminum, resembles wind-sculpted drifts of freshly laid snow—an effect that borders on the sublime in winter months when the whole landscape is white. The undulating forms continue inside the building. Visitors stepping into the lobby are met with a curvaceous, mesh-like glass curtain wall that soars up and overhead, and a grid-like structure of glass pyramids that glisten like crystals in bright sunlight. The theater itself is encased in sculpted panels of mellow Manchurian ash, countering the cool, wintry colors and motifs used outside. ∎

DESIGNER	MAD Architects
PROJECT	Harbin Opera House
LOCATION	Harbin

← The dramatic glass curtain walls undulate, as if billowed by the wind.

↙ The wood cladding the grand theater is "carved" to resemble an eroded block of wood.

↓ The grand theater, with its beautifully sculpted balcony and mezzanine seating.

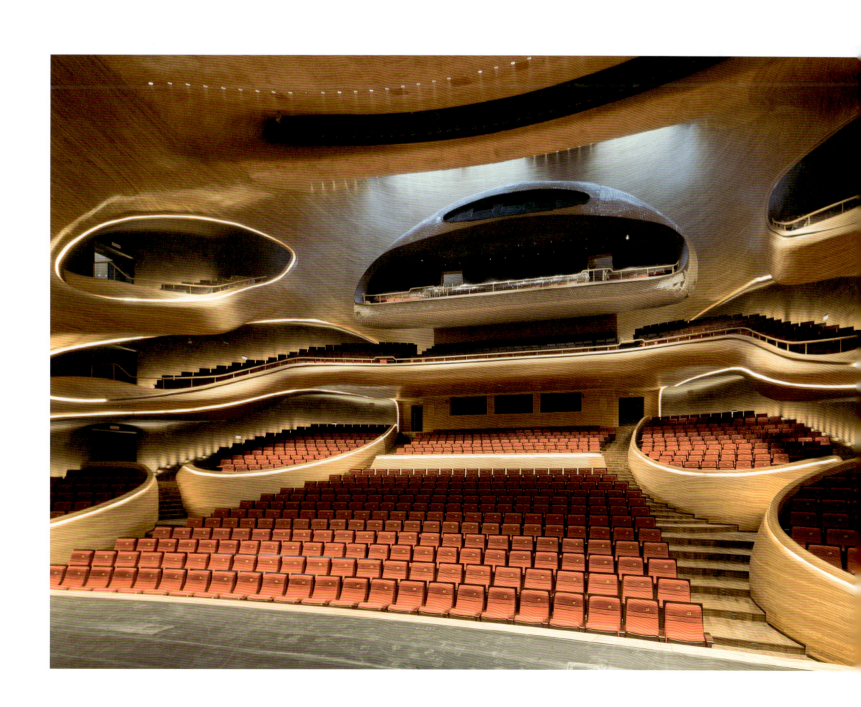

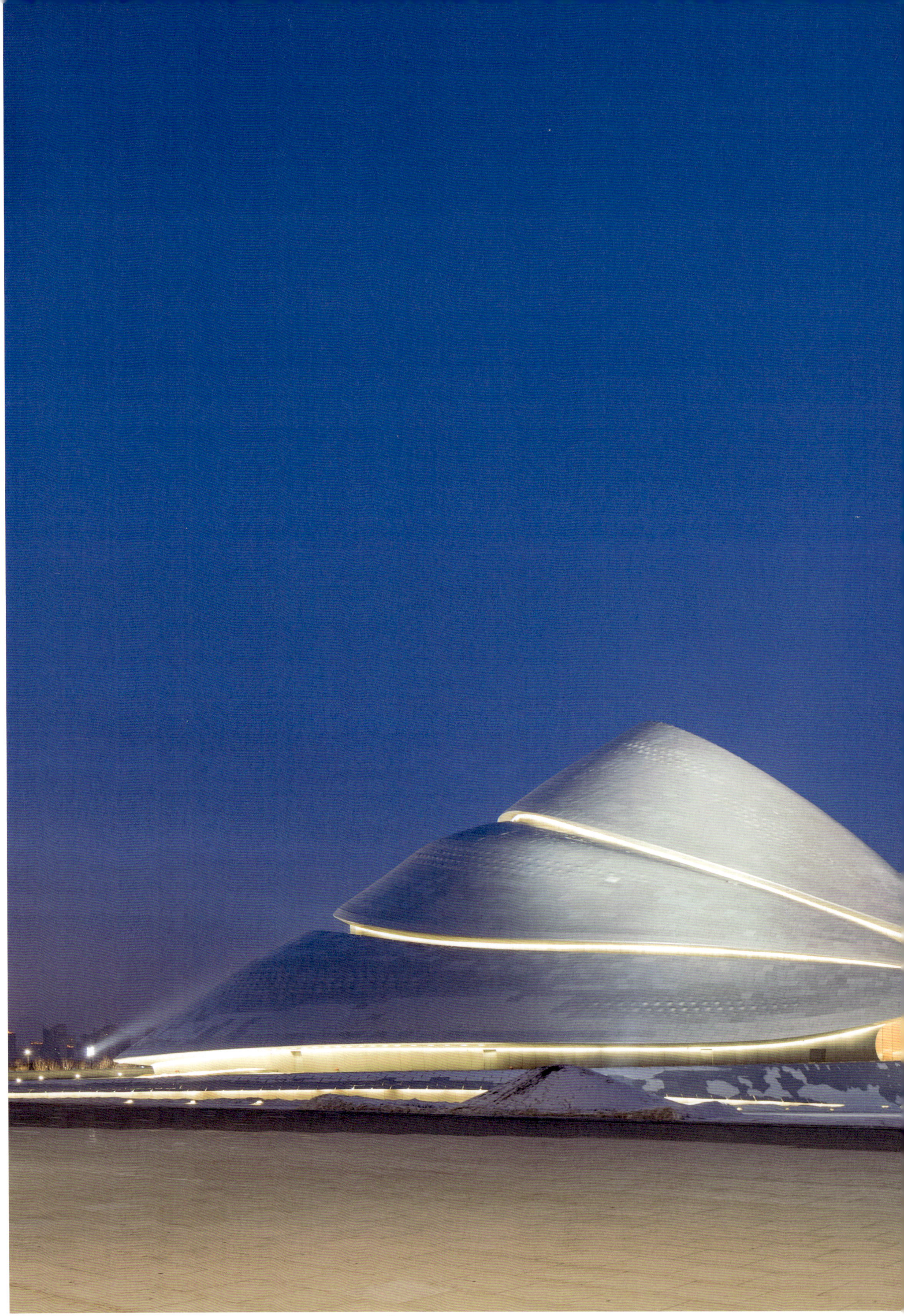

DESIGNER	CROX International
PROJECT	Liyang Museum
LOCATION	Liyang, Jiangsu Province

A Sinuous Form Inspired by a Traditional Musical Instrument

Dedicated to local history, Liyang Museum sits at the southeastern corner of Yan Lake Park in the new urban district of Liyang, a city in Jiangsu Province, north of Shanghai. The spectacular shape of the structure, designed by architects CROX International, was inspired by the profile of the surrounding mountains and the melodious tones of the *jiaoweiqin*, a traditional musical instrument, which is one of the city's cultural emblems. The fluid form, nestled into a series of undulating hills, is clad with narrow aluminum strips colored various shades of brown to resemble the carved wood of the stringed instrument. Inside, there are "past," "present," and "future" exhibition halls, and underneath, office, conference, and event spaces extend into the slopes below ground. The main entrance draws visitors in via a wooden stairway that leads up from an open courtyard below the building, while a second entrance encased in white concrete facing the lake is accessed from a stone path that winds its way around the perimeter of the site. A viewing gallery and a rooftop garden on top offer sweeping views across the lake, and, as night falls, a droplet-shaped terrace lights up, illuminating the sky above. Intended to function as a place for gathering and socializing for tourists and local residents alike, the cultural landmark is approachable and welcoming. ▐

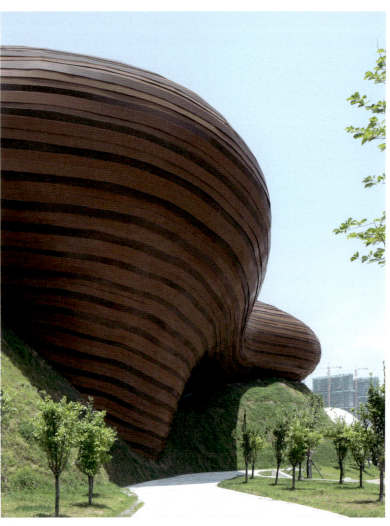

↑   The metal facade mimics the rich tones and textures of wood, but also captures the reflective qualities of a highly polished carved instrument.

→   The floating body of the museum makes physical contact with the landscape at just four points.

←   The organic shape of the museum blends and extends into the surrounding land, feeling natural and welcoming.

The museum's location beside a lake offers spectacular
views of the building from the surrounding landscape.

DESIGNER	MUDA-Architects
PROJECT	Garden Hotpot Restaurant
LOCATION	Chengdu

A Lakeside Restaurant that Dissolves into the Dense Forest Landscape

Skirting the edge of a misty lake and surrounded by a serene eucalyptus forest, Garden Hotpot Restaurant embodies the evolving environmentally conscious culture in Chengdu, in southwestern Sichuan Province. Located in the heart of the city's Sansheng Township, locally dubbed the "Chengdu green lung," the restaurant celebrates al fresco dining while preserving the ecology of the natural environment. Global architecture firm MUDA-Architects has taken great pains to minimize their intervention in this ancient landscape, opting to replace walls with lightweight structural pillars that allow the restaurant to dissolve into the forest beyond it. A noncorroding wooden floor creates a ribbon-like path along the edge of the lake, which is mirrored by the undulating steel roof overhead, preserving the natural lines of both the lake and forest. Wooden railings blur the boundary between the lake and the restaurant, bringing diners closer to nature and allowing them to enjoy spectacular views of the verdant landscape. The architects exploited the benefits of small-scale, low-cost architecture with this project. They developed a simple structure relying primarily on basic steel-welding techniques, reducing the overall construction time and costs. The result is a building that is light, transparent, and completely integrated with nature. ▮

An absence of walls allows the building to integrate
gently with the forest as it follows the curves of the lake.

DESIGNER	Emerge Architects
PROJECT	SINICA Eco Pavilion
LOCATION	Taipei, Taiwan

An Undulating Concrete Pavilion Blurs the Lines between Indoors and Out

The SINICA Eco Pavilion, located on the grounds of SINICA Academia, a major research facility in Taipei, Taiwan, serves as an information center, providing an important link between the institute and the nearby ecological pond, rice farm, and forest. The organic design developed by Taipei-based Emerge Architects was determined by the surrounding landscape, as the client was keen to preserve several mature trees growing around the site. The pavilion has a curved, almost amoebic form, defined by gaps in the vegetation, with four lobes of various sizes. The building, arranged on two floors, is constructed with large concrete floor slabs that extend beyond the line of the walls, which are made up of large sheets of glass interspersed with sections of perforated steel. At the heart of the pavilion, a full-height atrium brings natural light flooding into the interior spaces, casting leafy shadows that shift as the sun passes overhead. The fluid shape of the structure creates a seamless transition between the landscaped grounds, which seem to extend into the interiors. Strategic indoor planting adds to the effect, blurring the boundary between the inside and outside. Walking around the open structure, visitors pass through "pocket spaces" that signal the change of use between the reception, exhibition area, main hall, and so on. And with every step, the glass walls seem to melt away, evoking the sensation of taking a walk in the woods. ▍

→ There is a constant play of light and dark as natural light finds its way into the building.

↘ Wraparound glass ensures that the natural world is always visible.

↓ The large sweeping floor slabs with curvaceous overhanging edges make for a dynamic element of the design.

BACK TO THE COUNTRYSIDE: HOW CHINA'S HINTERLANDS ARE BEING REVITALIZED WITH MARKETS, LIBRARIES, AND HOTELS

For decades, China's modernization emphasized the growth of urban centers, with the countryside all but left behind. A new movement is rethinking rural areas to be a sustainable and serene contrast to the megacity.

In early February 2020, just before COVID-19 took New York City by storm, an exhibition titled *Countryside: The Future* opened at the Guggenheim Museum in the Upper East Side. Organized in collaboration with Rem Koolhaas and Samir Bantal from AMO—the think tank of the Office for Metropolitan Architecture (OMA)—the center-wide exhibition sought to put rural areas around the world at the center of discussions about the global future in the face of urban decay and accelerating climate change. A considerable proportion of the exhibition was dedicated to the Chinese countryside.

Koolhaas is certainly not alone when it comes to being interested in rural China. The early stages of China's modernization project following the reform and opening-up policies of 1978 largely focused on urbanization, but a marked shift in emphasis toward the potential of the country's rural heartlands has been underway for the past few years. However, this state-led rural reconstruction is not aimed at transforming rural villages into analogs of their urban counterparts along the coast. If anything, it is a response to the myriad consequences of China's urban acceleration over the past decades, which range from regional inequalities and soaring real estate prices in cities to environmental pollution and cultural homogenization, and aims to promote a more sustainable way of life as well as a more equitable relationship with nature. As part of this movement, a wave of Chinese architects has enthusiastically brought new projects to the hinterland.

For architect Xu Tiantian of the Beijing-based practice DnA Design and Architecture, innovative rural architecture has the power to help restore rural heritage and activate local economies. In January 2014, DnA began collaborating with Songyang County in southwest Zhejiang Province on what eventually developed

↑ DnA's Bamboo Pavilion at the Damushan Tea Plantation is a resting space for local tea farmers and tourists alike.

← The Tofu Factory by DnA is built on a slope following the river by the Caizhai Village entrance.

into a comprehensive revitalization plan consisting of more than 10 buildings located throughout the county's ancient villages, ranging from heritage museums and village centers to factories.

Adapting to a rural context, the urban design theory of architectural acupuncture proposes small-scale interventions as means of stimulating organic growth, as opposed to massive →

→ redevelopment. These buildings serve as catalysts that rejuvenate different sectors of the local economy. And just like acupuncture, which is a key component of traditional Chinese medicine, DnA's projects in Songyang involve various time-honored methods. Take the Bamboo Pavilion: built in the middle of the Damushan green tea field, a group of four pavilions, constructed entirely from locally sourced bamboo, provides tea plantation workers and visitors with a pit stop to rest and take in serene views of their surroundings. The pitched roofs provide shade from the intense sunlight and create the impression of a floating village when seen from a distance.

Organic Farm, designed by ARCHSTUDIO, uses timber for the main structure to reduce production costs.

The Tofu Factory is both a production and exhibition space of traditional heritage for Caizhai Village.

More recently, DnA built three new factories in Songyang to revitalize the surrounding rural economy. Among them, the Tofu Factory, a 13,000-square-foot (1,200-square-meter) wooden structure designed to bring Caizhai Village's famous tofu-making culture to a wider audience. The building, located on a slope along the river close to the village entrance, is divided into six sections according to function. Visitors ascending the stairs can observe the production process, step-by-step, before finally arriving in the tasting hall to dig in. The factory's design celebrates the village's cultural heritage by transforming the previously behind-the-scenes manufacturing process into theater, putting the villagers' craftsmanship center stage. DnA's Songyang initiatives have helped inject the region with vital energy while also restoring its residents' confidence in their future.

As the breadbasket of China's enormous population, the countryside plays an extraordinarily important role in the nation's agricultural supply chain. However, decades of rural-to-urban migration—due to the higher quality of life in cities compared to the precarious working conditions for farmers—have drained the countryside of talent in the agricultural sector. →

The structure of the factory creates a dialogue with the wooden structures of old farmhouses in the village.

The design is inspired by traditional courtyard architecture and creates functional areas of different sizes under one big roof.

The early stages of China's modernization focused on urbanization, but a marked shift in emphasis toward the potential of the country's rural heartlands has been underway for the past few years.

With the development of a stronger rural economy in some parts of China, newly affluent villagers are also eager to bring home modern, cutting-edge design to which architects have responded enthusiastically.

→ These factors have improved agricultural infrastructure, one of the most crucial goals of rural reconstruction, and architects have made considerable strides in recent years. Completed in 2016, ARCHSTUDIO's Tangshan Organic Farm is located in Tangshan's Guye District. Serving as a processing facility, it collects, processes, and packs raw materials from organic farms across the country before shipping them out as finished products. The 65,000-square-foot (6,000-square-meter) facility resembles a supersized traditional courtyard composed of four volumes that serve as the storage depot, mill, oil pressing facility, and packing area, leaving an empty field in the middle where produce can be sun-dried. The use of timber for the roof, frame, and flooring, and PVC board for the walls reduces construction costs and gives the site a luminous and welcoming atmosphere.

Vector Architects added concrete reinforcement to the original brick masonry walls and reconfigured the internal layout.

Following a destructive earthquake in 2014 in Guangming, rammed earth is used to build safe homes for villagers.

Vector Architects included a third floor with a vaulted ceiling to the existing structure of Captain's House.

In Guangming, a prototype house has been built for an elderly couple to validate the building the technology and performance.

By improving rural farmers' working conditions, innovative industrial architecture like ARCHSTUDIO's organic farm hopes to attract urban migrants back to the countryside, anticipating a revitalized agrarian culture.

Meanwhile, other initiatives have focused on improving housing conditions in rural villages. Located between the world's two largest seismic belts, many parts of China are at high risk of earthquakes. These areas with heightened seismic activity largely overlap with the most remote and mountainous regions of China, where the prevalence of low-quality buildings—many constructed in violation of building codes—makes them even more vulnerable. In 2014, an earthquake of magnitude 6.1 →

The main building of the Heduli Paddy Hotel is rebuilt from disused primary school buildings.

→ on the Richter scale shattered tens of thousands of homes in Ludian County in Yunnan, a province in southwest China. Post-earthquake, the residents of Guangming Village realized they needed to rebuild their homes with more structural resilience, but they could not afford the higher-quality materials they required. In response, the Chinese University of Hong Kong collaborated with Kunming University of Science and Technology to develop an improved, affordable rammed-earth building system and constructed a prototype house for an elderly couple to demonstrate its validity. It features steel bars and concrete belts built into walls composed of a new formula using clay, sand, grass, and other local, cost-effective materials, thereby improving seismic performance. Double-paned windows and insulated roofs are incorporated into the design to enhance insulation. The low cost and relatively simple procedures also guarantee that local villagers can learn the technologies themselves, acquiring skills that qualify them to find work in future rural reconstruction projects.

A growing number of urban dwellers are beginning to see the countryside in a new light, thanks to the many boutique hotels and guesthouses that have opened in rural villages in recent years. The Heduli Paddy Hotel by C&C Design in Hedu Village in Huizhou is a case in point. Transforming an abandoned primary school and employing locally sourced materials such as bamboo and tiles throughout, the eco-friendly hotel offers visitors the opportunity to relax and enjoy the tranquil setting while developing a deeper appreciation for the rural way of life on a weekend retreat.

With the development of a stronger rural economy in some parts of China, newly affluent villagers are also eager to bring home modern, cutting-edge design—once an exclusively urban luxury—to which architects have responded enthusiastically. The renovation of a sea captain's house on the southeastern end of Huangqi Peninsula in Fujian Province by Beijing-based practice Vector Architects exemplifies this trend. Twenty years of standing beside the sea had left the original structure suffering from severe water damage. After assessing the building's condition, Dong Gong of Vector Architects added concrete reinforcement to the original brick masonry walls and

The building appears to be growing out of the rice fields, allowing guests to return to a rural life.

reconfigured the internal layout. The bedrooms were moved to the side facing the sea, welcoming in more natural light and fresh air. Protruding window frames set into the outside wall create extra space while functioning as a desk and viewing station. An extra floor was added on top of the building, providing space for exercise and family gatherings, topped with a barrel vault to channel rain. The elegant and functional design has transformed a once-ordinary village house into a deluxe villa, nothing short of a resort getaway, adding an exquisite landmark to the Huangqi coastline.

With top-down and bottom-up initiatives supported by homegrown architects, the countryside—once dismissed as backward and uninspiring—is experiencing a much-deserved renaissance. As novel architecture emerges across rural China, we may not be all that far from a time when everyone dreams of moving out of tired cities to the countryside. ∎

C&C Design uses a large number of local materials such as bamboo, river stones, bricks, and tiles.

The reconstruction of rural areas is a response to the myriad consequences of China's urban acceleration over the past decades, and aims to promote a more sustainable way of life as well as a more equitable relationship with nature.

By improving rural farmers' working conditions, innovative industrial architecture hopes to attract urban migrants back to the countryside, anticipating a revitalized agrarian culture.

DESIGNER	Atelier tao+c
PROJECT	Capsule Hotel and Bookstore
LOCATION	Qinglongwu Village, Tonglu, Zhejiang Province

A Dual-Purpose Development Evolves from Building within a Building

Nestled in the ancient village of Qinglongwu, against the mountainous green backdrop of Huaxi Forest Park, this capsule hotel and bookstore is the creative work of Shanghai-based architects Atelier tao+c. "Creative" is the right word, for almost the only thing that remains of the original structure is the timber-framed shell and its mud walls. Even then, the entire gable wall at the eastern end of the building has been replaced with a transparent structure of wooden frames and corrugated polycarbonate panels to maximize views of the verdant landscape. Inside the building, Atelier tao+c removed the original floors and partition walls and remodeled the space to house two independent floating volumes inside it. Each of these volumes—one for men and one for women—contains 10 identical capsule bedrooms and a shared bathroom. There is a neat balance between the privacy of the accommodation and the openness of the surrounding public spaces. At 4.4 feet (1.35 meters) tall, the ceiling height of the sleeping accommodation only allows guests to sit or to lie down but frees up space to split the rest of the space into three floors with staggered walkways and mezzanines. The result is a collection of public spaces with an intriguing mix of triple- and double-height areas connected by thin metal staircases. Zigzagging routes echo mountain paths, and offer spots for meandering, ascending, resting, reading, or simply taking in the view. ∎

↑   The split and stacked floors are connected by thin metal staircases with just nine steps between levels.

←   Window sizes are based on the grid-like module of the library shelves within.

→   The transparent gable end combines with openings in the ceiling to bring natural light into the interior.

A Hotel Complex Echoes the Surrounding Village Vernacular

Lying to the south of Beigou Village, which is considered to be one of China's most beautiful settlements, San Sa is hotel development with a twist. Arranged as a cluster of brick "dwellings" connected by a series of narrow walkways and terraces, the resort seeks to subvert the norms of the leisure industry. Shanghai-based architects llLab. describe it as a "village within a village." Each "house" provides a combination of private bedrooms, courtyards, and communal spaces for dining and socializing, in a semi-rural landscape planted with trees. According to llLab., the aim is to provide guests with "a spatial and sensory experience that evokes personal renewal by reflecting on the imagined memory of lives past." To achieve this, the architects took elements from the traditional village architecture commonly found further north and replicated it using authentic and readily available local resources: stone slabs for paving, old slate tiles for roofs, and brickwork for courtyards. The exterior walls rise from rough stonework at the base to neat sections of red or blue brickwork above, as if the new emerges from the old. Aside from the texture and color of the building materials, there are no ornamental or decorative elements. Inside, the rooms are also spare and neutral with white-plastered walls and dark timber floors. The "houses" are arranged in an irregular pattern to replicate the organic growth of a traditional village with one- and two-story units jostling for space and oriented to face different directions. There is an air of harmony and tranquility, making San Sa a place of contemplation for those seeking to escape from everyday life, offering a chance to find the time and space to recharge the mind, body, and spirit. ▌

DESIGNER	llLab.
PROJECT	San Sa Village
LOCATION	Beigou Village, Huairou District

↑ The development follows the slope of the land so that some dwellings are naturally higher up than others.

← The random arrangement of the dwellings allows for numerous private outdoor patios and terraces.

↓ The generous rooms are reminiscent of remote mountain retreats.

↑ Low lighting in the rooms combines with the neutral color scheme to create deeply restful spaces.

← Everything, from bathroom fittings to external spaces, is kept to a human scale in a bid to enhance the guests' sense of well-being.

→ As dusk falls and lights begin to come on across the complex, it really does capture the "village" atmosphere.

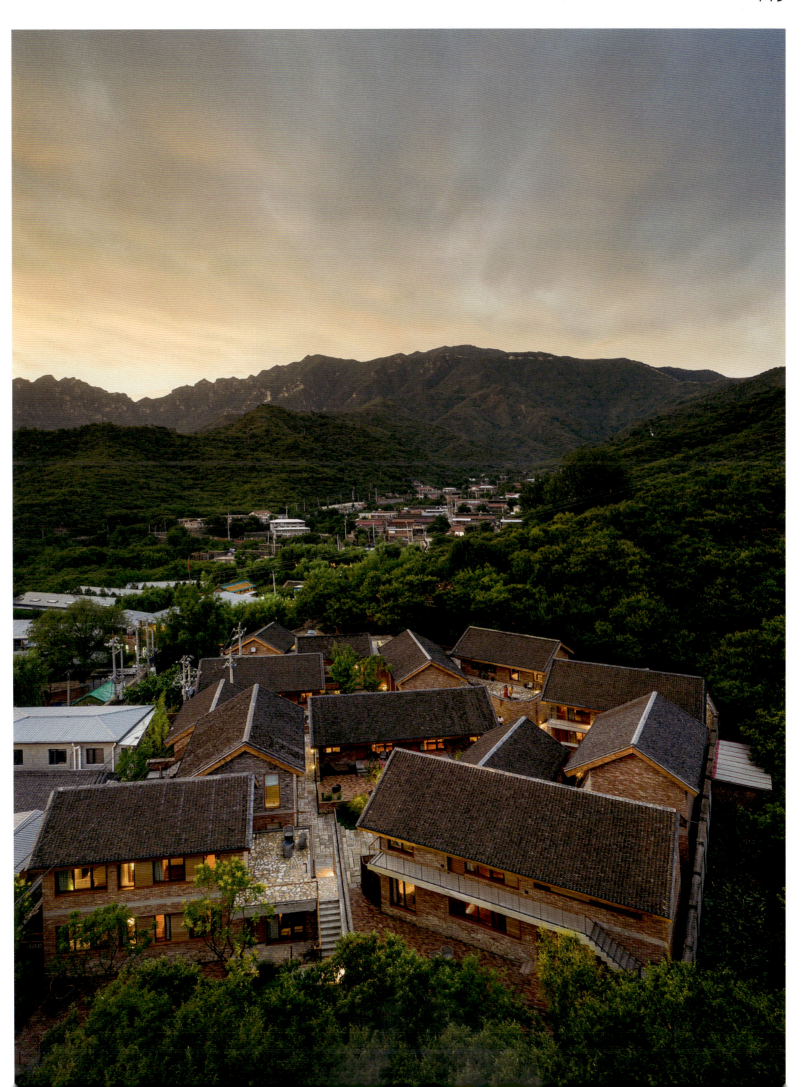

DESIGNER	Atelier cnS / South China University of Technology
PROJECT	Public Toilets in Zuzhai Village
LOCATION	Tangkou Town, Kaiping, Guangdong Province

Bolstering Rural Village Life through the Regeneration of a Communal Amenity

In rural China, it's not a given that every home has a household toilet. Therefore, public restrooms have to function as an attractive amenity for the community as a whole, while affording users the privacy most of us can expect at home. Addressing these seemingly contradictory qualities lies at the heart of Atelier cnS's design for public toilets for a village community in Tangkou Town, Kaiping. Their design achieves the right balance with the introduction of three novel elements: landscape steps, a semicircular wall, and the repurposing of old materials. The first, a wide staircase with built-in bench seating, leads up to a platform above the toilet block, which is the focal point of the design. It conceals the public toilets below and roots the building into the local infrastructure by providing villagers with a place to congregate. The second element—the curved wall—blurs the boundary between the inside and outside space by creating three courtyards that open onto the surrounding landscape. Each of the courtyards encompass a tree—one of them a century-old mango tree. And the third novel element lies in the fabric of the walls themselves, which are constructed from wire-cage modules filled with fragments of broken brick, stone, clay, and tile salvaged from demolitions in the village. They are stacked one on top of the other, with the most densely packed at the bottom to support the building's weight. Toward the top of the wall, the cages are less tightly packed and contain shards of crockery—and even a whole teapot—reinforcing the sense of community that the design seeks to arouse in local residents. █

→ The semicircle wall eases the transition from outside to inside and from public to private.

↘ The wire-cage modules are spaced to allow maximum natural light and ventilation into the block without compromising on privacy.

↓ The raised platform floats above the toilet block, overhanging the main volume.

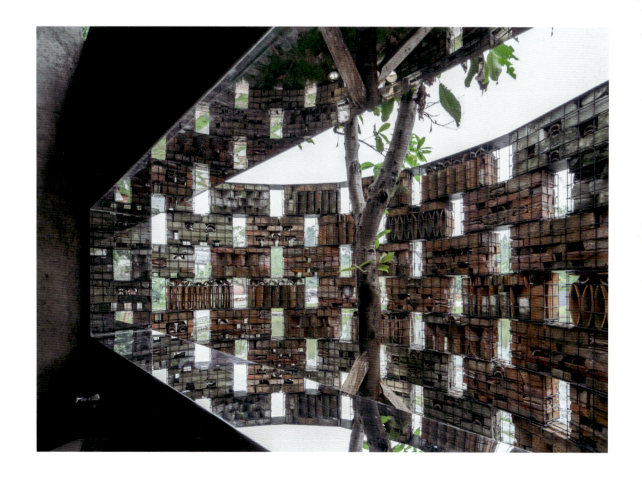

DESIGNER	One Take Architects
PROJECT	Shelter · The Mirrored Sight
LOCATION	Longli, Jinping, Kaili Area, Guizhou

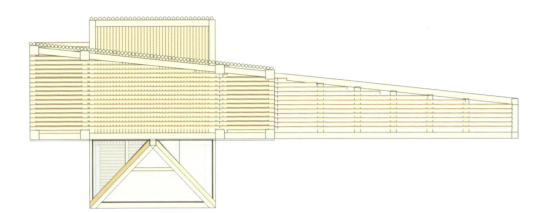

A Lone Riverside Shelter Offers Rest and Respite for One Guest at a Time

This curious shelter sits on the north bank of Longxi River overlooking the old town of Longli in Jinping County, in Guizhou province. Intriguingly named Shelter · The Mirrored Sight and designed by One Take Architects, the tall, narrow structure has two levels: an upper gallery from which people can enjoy views of the immediate surroundings, and a lower floor with accommodations for one guest. While the skin of the northern facade is crafted from local bamboo, the southern facade is clad with mirrored glass. The glass reflects scenes from the city on the opposite bank of the river and the half-pyramid form of the shelter. Intended to serve as a place for rest and respite, the photogenic design has turned the shelter into a regional land-mark. When night falls, it takes on a somewhat surreal appearance, as the overall shape of the structure blends with the darkness, the "pyramid" appears to float in mid-air. This is just one of several contrasts associated with the shelter. While it overlooks Longli, it clearly does not belong to the town. The town itself is home to thousands of residents, while the shelter accommodates just one. People in the town go about their everyday lives, while those staying at the shelter enjoy a once-in-a-lifetime experience. Sitting on the edge of historic Longli, the shelter stands isolated, marking the division between the town and the rural landscape. ▮

DESIGNER	LUO Studio
PROJECT	Party and Public Service Center
LOCATION	Yuanheguan Village, Hubei Province

An Invaluable Community Space Built in a Matter of Months

When the community hall in Yuanheguan Village was repurposed to serve as the hub for a pilot tourism scheme in the Wudang Mountain area of Hubei Province, it was necessary to find new premises for the villagers to assemble. Given the challenge of creating a new center in just two months, the architects at LUO Studio identified a plot where the foundations of a previously abandoned construction would give them a head start. Building on the existing steel-reinforced concrete framework, LUO Studio opted to use wood as the primary material. Not only was this in keeping with the local vernacular, but it offered the benefits of speedy assembly through prefabrication. The first floor is enclosed by a perforated wall built with gray clay and glass bricks, and the second floor is almost entirely constructed with exposed wooden beams and paneling. The center's rooms are large and predominantly open plan, and a skylight runs along the length of the pitched roof, flooding the building with natural daylight. Outside, to the south side of the building, a terrace over-looks the village and a Taoist temple, with views of the mountains rising in the distance, and on the west side of the building there is a casual meeting spot with public notice boards and a long wooden bench backing onto the gray brick wall. With this space and the building's inviting interior, the architects have provided the villagers with a shared environment to establish more intimate interpersonal and community relationships. ∎

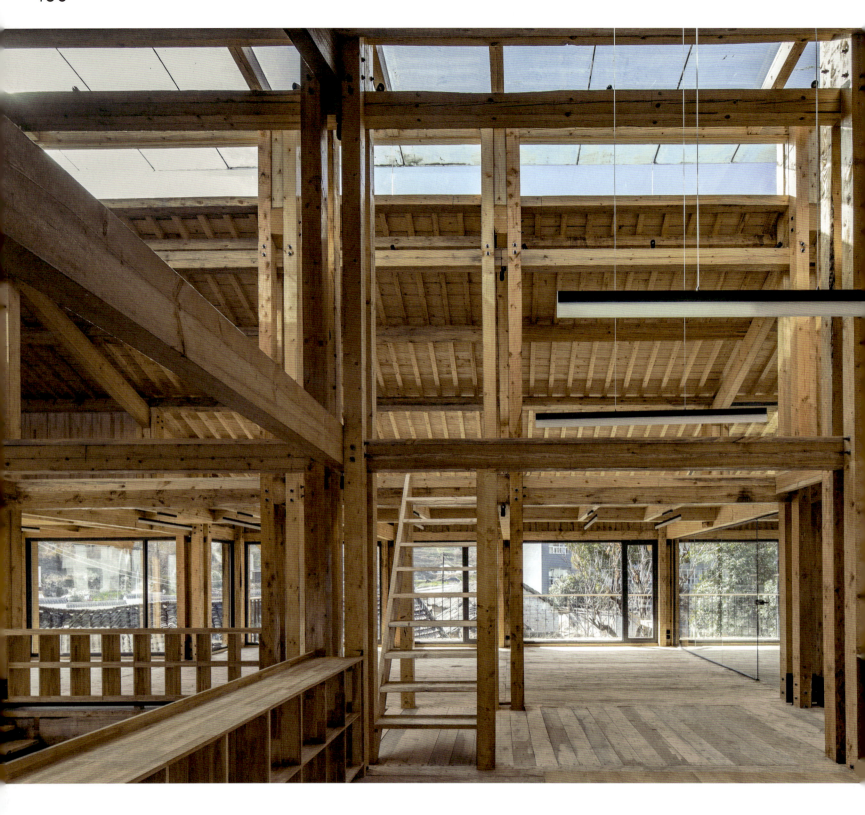

↑   On the second floor, large areas of floor-to-ceiling
windows provide good views to the outside.

→   The long overhang on the roof suggests a modern
interpretation of the vernacular architecture.

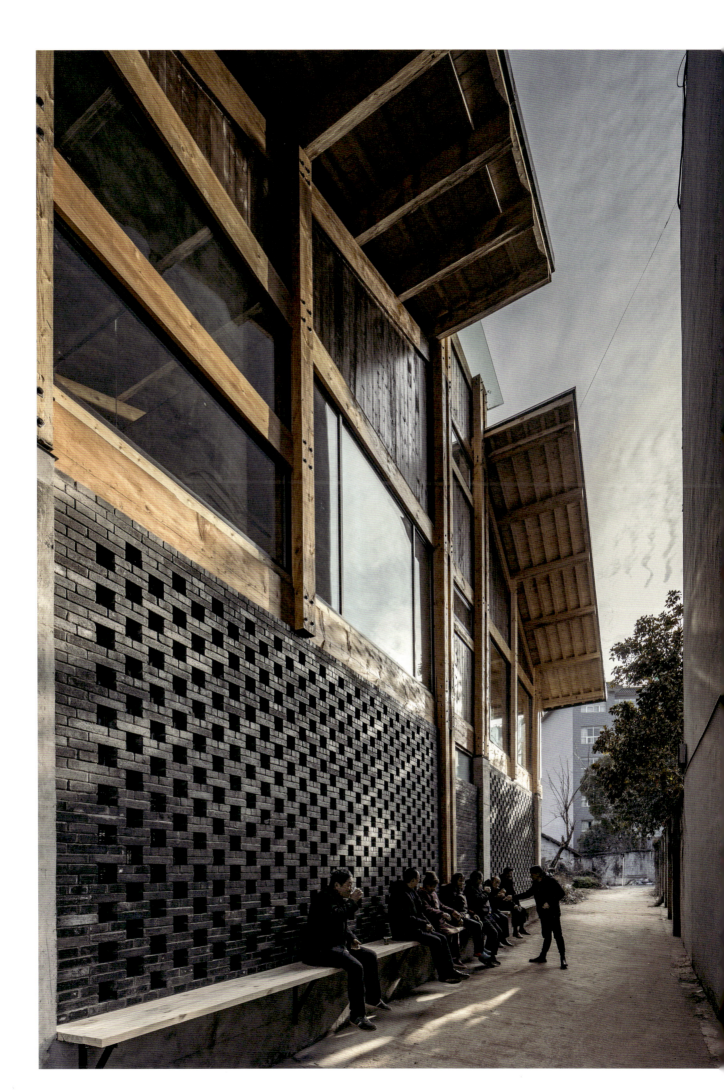

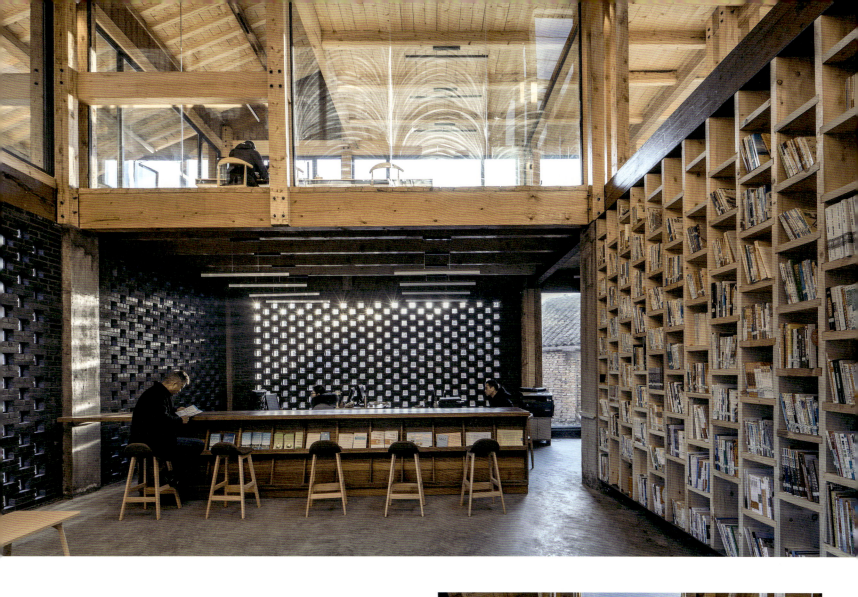

↑ The open-plan layout incorporates numerous smaller spaces for seating, reading, and assembling in groups.

← On the first floor, light filters in through the glass bricks interwoven with the gray masonry bricks.

→ Additional light enters the building through the long skylight in the roof.

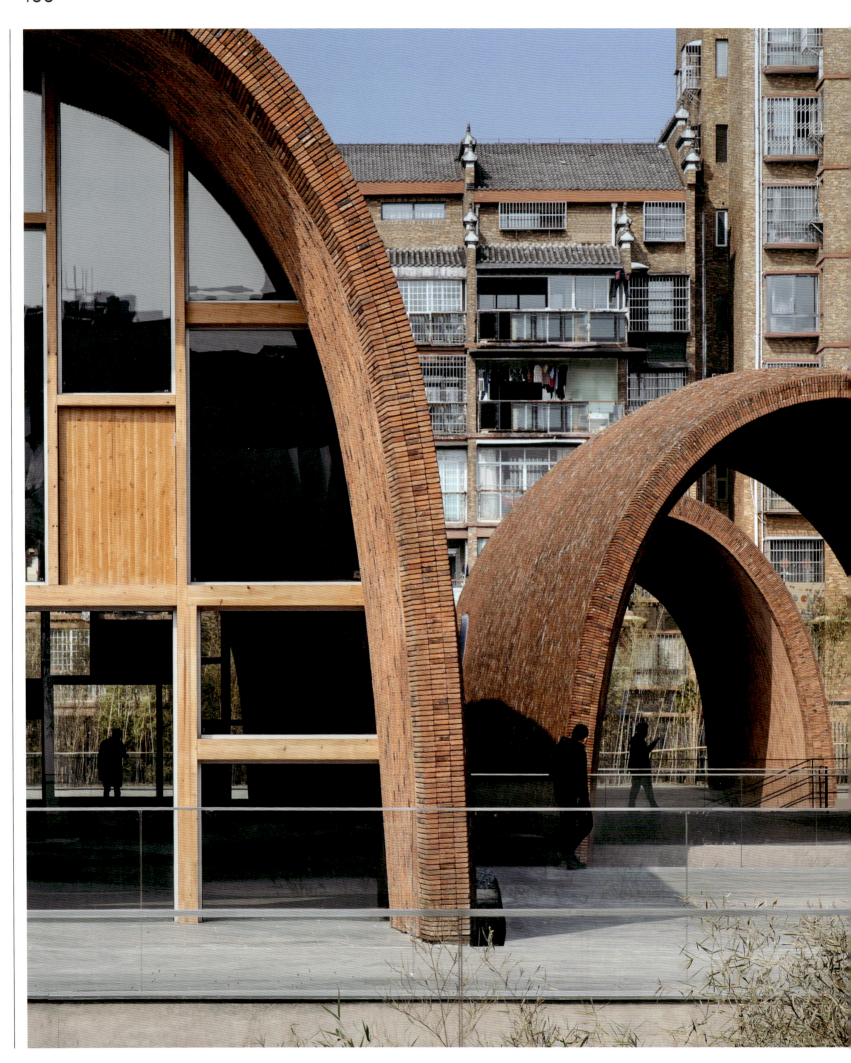

RETHINKING THE ROLE OF TRADITIONAL ARCHITECTURE FOLLOWING DECADES OF "DEMOLISH AND REBUILD"

Traditional architecture can be hard to define in a territory as vast as this one. And yet, following the sweeping urbanization of the past three decades, a revival of historic forms and techniques is emerging.

After 40 years of wide-ranging economic reform and integration with the global market, China has largely accomplished modernization and is now seeking a new cultural identity. In the pursuit of a fitting style of architecture for the 21st century, Chinese architects have turned back to tradition, much of which was lost in the course of rapid development. What is the essence of traditional Chinese architecture? And how can it be adapted to a contemporary context, given the complex and fast-changing nature of Chinese cities?

Traditional Chinese architecture resists simplistic characterization, especially considering the multifaceted role it played in ancient China. Architecture is an integral part of Confucian philosophy, the ideology dominant in China for over 2,000 years. Buildings were planned and constructed following *li* (rituals) by the vast imperial bureaucracy following instructions from the emperor, who believed it was a vital aspect of his "Mandate of Heaven." Despite traditional Chinese architecture's complexity and diversity, it is possible to identify some recurring traits and motifs in the surviving timber structures: mortise-and-tenon joints; overhanging, concave, tile-clad roofs; and the harmonious integration of buildings with their surroundings.

There is no denying that an appreciation of traditional architecture is part of the Chinese people's collective unconscious. Its influence is evident in the Chinese way of dwelling and arrangement of the space today, whether at the interior or urban scale. However, as a result of a stringent "demolish and rebuild" model enacted in the name of urban renewal, many of China's modern cities have a similar appearance. Returning to the roots of Chinese architecture offers an alternative view to the generic cityscapes.

↑ Traditional architecture in Beijing, with modern high-rises in the distance.

← For the Imperial Kiln Museum, Studio Zhu-Pei designed an eye-catching arched structure that echoes the shape of old kilns.

Architects worldwide have experimented with combining regional traditions and features with modernist idealism, and Chinese architects are no exception—mostly notably the architect and scholar Liang Sicheng, who is known as the father of Chinese architecture. Liang, along with his partner, the architect and →

→ poet Lin Huiyin, was among the first Chinese students to study architecture overseas in the 1920s at Harvard and the University of Pennsylvania. During the Japanese occupation (1931–1945), Liang and Lin traveled around war-torn China to identify and document 2,000 ancient buildings. Some of their most significant discoveries were Foguang Temple, Yingzhou Pagoda, and Zhaozhou Bridge.

The Shenzhen area has undergone rapid modernization and was one of the fastest-growing cities in the world.

The capricious political campaigns of socialist China prevented Liang from realizing his ambition of modernizing Chinese architecture. In the early 1950s, there was a heated debate between planners from the Soviet Union and Chinese experts like Liang Sicheng, about the fate of the old city of Beijing as part of the process of building a new capital. Liang's plan was to leave it untouched and rebuild a new city center in the outskirts. However, the party eventually chose a production-centric, cost-effective plan: they demolished large parts of the old city and repurposed the rest, with factories built inside the city. Caught in the air pollution and traffic congestion plaguing the capital today, Beijing residents still lament Liang's defeat and later persecution during the Cultural Revolution, but Liang's idealism didn't completely die out.

In 2012, Hangzhou-based architect Wang Shu became the first Chinese citizen to win the Pritzker Prize. In a sense, Wang's rise to international acclaim marked a contemporary renaissance of traditional Chinese architecture. "The question of the proper relation of present to past is particularly timely, for the recent process of urbanization in China invites debate as to whether architecture should be anchored in tradition or

should look only toward the future," said Pritzker Prize jury chairman Peter Palumbo on Wang's award. "As with any great architecture, Wang Shu's work is able to transcend that debate, producing an architecture that is timeless, deeply rooted in its context and yet universal."

Wang and his partner and wife Lu Wenyu founded Amateur Architecture Studio in 1998. They named their studio as such because they were critical of the Chinese architectural profession, which they viewed as complicit in the demolition of entire urban areas at that time. Wang's commitment to traditional craftsmanship and cultural continuity has manifested

For the Xiangshan Campus, Wang Shu and Lu Wenyu mixed traditional architecture with contemporary elements.

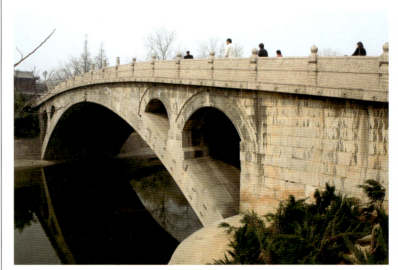

The Zhaozhou Bridge is the world's oldest open-spandrel segmental arch bridge of stone construction.

itself throughout his career. From 1990 to 1998, when he was not working on commissions, he lived and worked with local artisans to learn traditional building techniques, something few other architects are willing to do. Historically, construction knowledge has been passed on orally from mentor to pupil, so working directly with builders was the only way of →

In the pursuit of a fitting style of architecture for the
21st century, Chinese architects have turned back to tradition,
much of which was lost in the course of rapid development.

Wang Shu became the first Chinese citizen to win the Pritzker Prize.
His rise to international acclaim marked a contemporary renaissance
of traditional Chinese architecture.

The Imperial Kiln Museum comprises more than half a dozen brick vaults based on the traditional form of the kiln.

→ learning the craft. Wang's unusual trajectory has made him an outlier, but his unique experience of time-honored building methods gives him a profound understanding of traditional architecture.

In 2004, Wang and Lu designed the Xiangshan Campus of the China Academy of Arts in Hangzhou, and the resulting structures are equally refreshing. The 19.7-acre (8-hectare) campus forms a self-contained town, which curves along the base of a hill. Students live and study in a cohesive collection of buildings with bamboo-panel facades, perforated brick walls, and elegantly curved roofs. Wang's signature use of locally sourced and recycled materials offers a fresh perspective on traditional forms and building techniques, and the campus has a strong relationship with the surrounding landscape. The buildings are nestled into the site, responding to the undulating terrain.

In 2008, after a series of renovation projects, Wang and Lu completed their masterpiece, the Ningbo Historic Museum. Built from traditional materials such as ceramic tiles and bamboo, it celebrates Ningbo's regional history and customs inside and out. Depending on the viewer's perspective, the asymmetric volume appears either mountain-like or boat-shaped, referencing Ningbo's history as a port city. The building's most notable feature is the facade constructed from millions of recycled bricks and tiles salvaged from the demolition of local buildings. Recycling construction material, and, in particular, gray bricks, is a long-standing practice in China. Wang's material palette turns the museum into a sort of Ship of Theseus and an urban icon of Ningbo. He briefed the builders personally during the construction process, giving them loose instructions and the freedom to carry out brick-laying techniques using independent judgment. This approach has delivered an intriguing facade with a rich, organic appearance, bridging the gap between past and present.

Several other new museums that pay homage to the country's complex history have been built in recent years, many of which incorporate reclaimed materials. Studio Zhu-Pei's Jingdezhen Imperial Kiln Museum is a tribute to Jingdezhen's long history as China's porcelain production center. The museum takes the form of an array of brick arches based on the traditional shape of a kiln. As is common in the local area, the volumes of varying size and curvature were partially built from reclaimed bricks from local kilns, creating a series of inviting spaces that reflect the area's heritage.

SUP Atelier's scheme for the History Museum of Qifeng Village is smaller scale, but no less ambitious. Typical of the practice's preservationist approach to renovation, they transformed a dilapidated house into a modern exhibition space that embodies the local area's history and character by retaining the original building's intricate wooden structure.

Jishou Art Museum by Beijing-based architects Atelier FCJZ highlights the architectural heritage of China's ethnic minorities. Jishou was the capital of Xiangxi, an autonomous zone for Tujia people. The museum's form takes inspiration from the traditional *fengyu qiao* style of bridge, the earliest example of which dates back 2,000 years. This type of bridge offered shelter from poor weather, as well as spaces for relaxation and gatherings. Atelier FCJZ's scheme houses a two-story art museum and functions as a transit route across the river, allowing local residents to encounter art as they commute across the city for work or leisure.

After the struggle of Liang Sicheng's era and the experimentation of Wang Shu's generation, revisiting traditional architecture amid China's ongoing urbanization remains highly contested. The current commodification of nostalgia and the politicization of culture and heritage present further challenges for architects exploring this route. After all, the revival of the past is not just about the past; it is also about the here and now. ▮

SUP Atelier transformed a dilapidated house into a modern exhibition space for the History Museum of Qifeng.

The current commodification of nostalgia and the politicization of culture and heritage present further challenges for architects exploring this route.

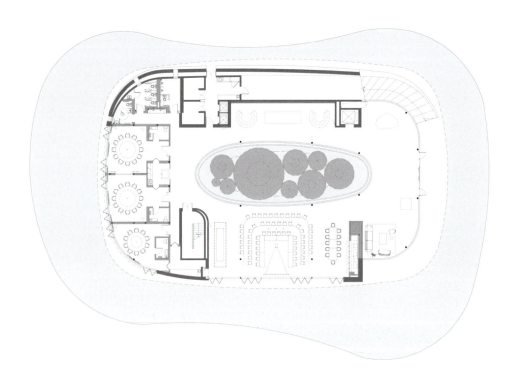

In Sichuan Province, a Community Center Inspired by Calligraphy and Centuries-Old Poetry

The Inkstone House OCT Linpan Cultural Center in Anren, shares a deep synergy with its surroundings. Its location in Sichuan Province, close to the Qimu River, surrounded by vast fields and bamboo forests, tells half the story while tradition accounts for the rest. Shanghai-based architectural design firm Archi-Union Architects integrated elements of the natural landscape with those of the vernacular architecture and the region's cultural history—specifically a poem titled *Passing by Anren* by Song Dynasty poet Huang Jian. Inspiration for the form of the cultural center came from the shape of the inkstones used traditionally for Chinese calligraphy. The gently curved rectangular structure is hollow at the center, creating an enclosed courtyard. The ground floor, rendered in dark-gray brick, acts as a solid and stable base while the upper level is slightly recessed and features soaring floor-to-ceiling windows that form a ring around the entire level. The undulating slate-tiled roof sweeps dramatically down into the oval-shaped courtyard, where it hovers above a series of large circular pools of water. Inside, the ground floor is equipped with exhibition space, a reception area, a conference room, and communication facilities, while the floor above houses an array of multipurpose rooms of different sizes for tea tasting, musical performances, dining, and playing chess. A sinuous path connects the center with an agricultural building used mainly to store farm equipment, which stands a short distance away. The walkway appears to float just above the ground, preserving the habitat for local flora and fauna while encouraging the flow of villagers and tourists. ▌

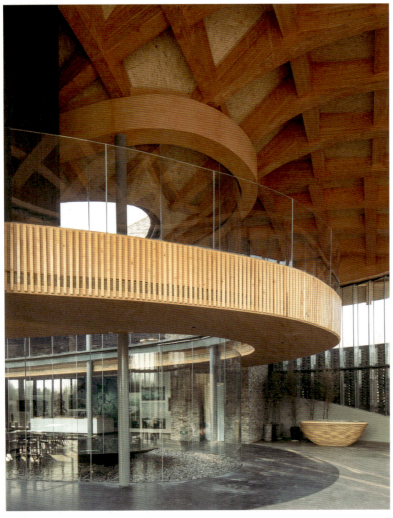

↑   Furnishings within the building echo the neutral browns, grays, and black of the primary building materials.

→   In the words of Archi-Union Architects founder Philip F. Yuan, the elegant curve of the building seeks to connect the boundary of the sky and the earth.

←   The architects employed digital fabrication methods to create distinctly contemporary and sculptural forms within the building.

→ Interior spaces are flooded with natural light, thanks to the generous amount of wraparound windows.

↘ The corridor snaking across the landscape mirrors shapes and materials found inside the main building.

↓ The building offers a contemporary interpretation of traditional Chinese architecture, essentially a stable base that supports a pedestal roof.

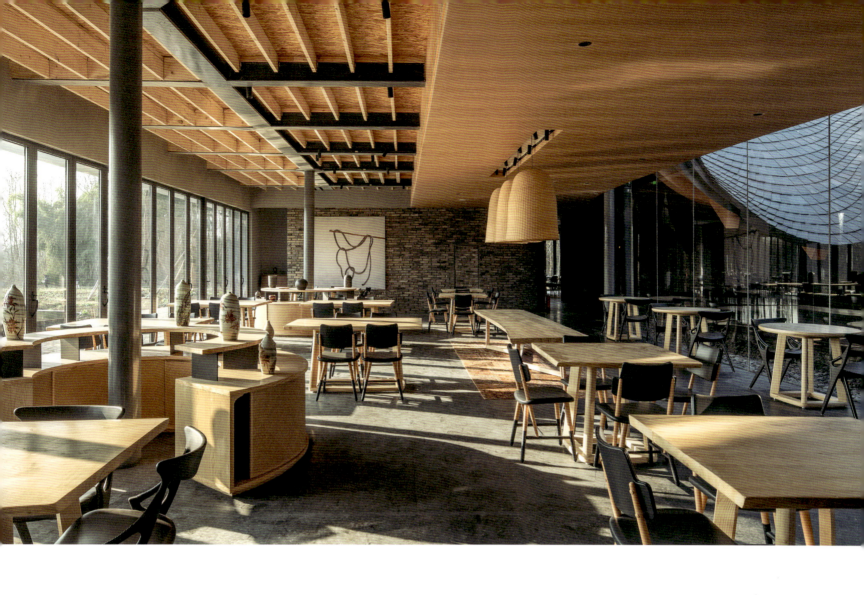

Exploring the Impact of Small Interventions in an Existing Architectural Space

This renovation sees a traditional courtyard house transformed into a multipurpose studio providing accommodation as well as working and exhibition space for a young artist. The dwelling occupies one of four volumes flanking a typical domestic courtyard in the Dashilan district of Beijing. With just 1,600 square feet (150 square meters) of interior space at their disposal, architectural firm hyperSity had to be creative. The building had been expanded during a prior refurbishment, but the team was able to further increase the overall footprint with a series of clever interventions. A high, perforated gray brick wall extends into the courtyard, creating a private outdoor space that runs the full length of the building. Behind this is a glass facade, which is shielded by a wooden grille, ensuring that natural light flows into the home while maintaining privacy. To increase space inside the dwelling, the architects utilized the attic to add a second story. They also removed a section of the ceiling on the first floor to form a double-height space that can be used for living, coworking, and exhibitions. On the ground floor, a series of strawboard structures divide the interior to improve efficiency and create separate areas for the kitchen, bathroom, laundry room, office, tatami room, and restroom. All in all, the architects have made a series of relatively small changes, yet they have expanded the building's utility manifold. ▮

DESIGNER	hyperSity Architects
PROJECT	V House of Dashilar
LOCATION	Beijing

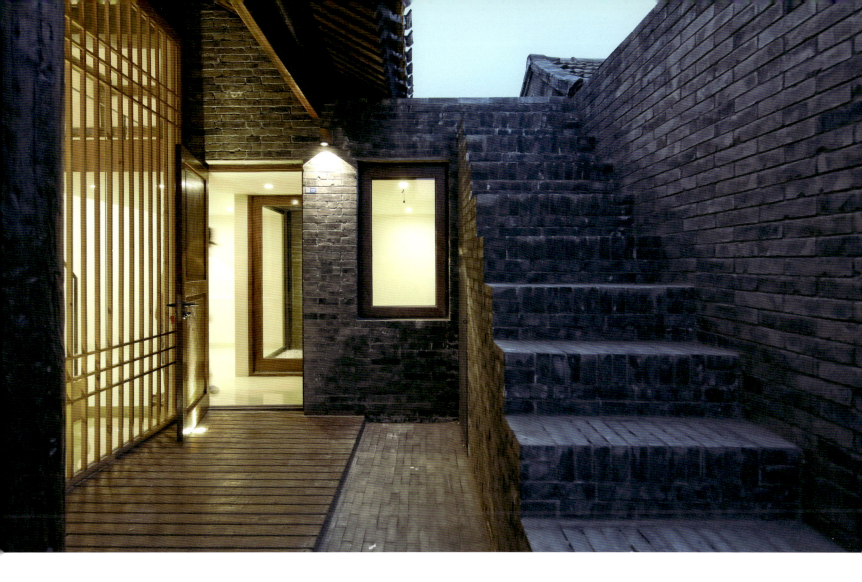

↑   Across the open courtyard, a flight of external stairs leads to a small roof terrace.

←   The central strawboard structure incorporates several small built-in areas for private work and sit-down group discussion.

→   While ensuring residents a degree of internal privacy, the perforated wall structure also increases transparency for looking out.

DESIGNER	Urbanus
PROJECT	Quad of Gourd
LOCATION	Beijing

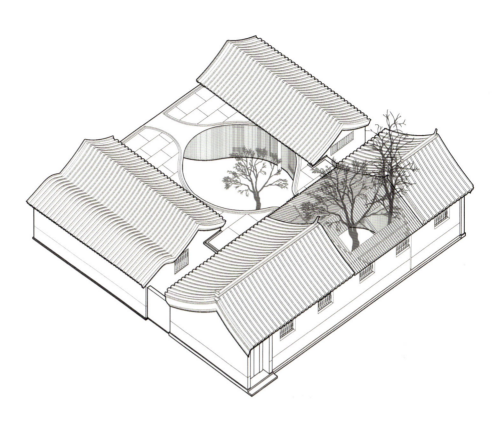

Embracing an Evolving Urban Landscape While Respecting the Passage of Time

When Beijing and Shenzhen-based architectural design practice Urbanus took on this renovation project in Beijing's residential Luanqing Hutong district, very little of the original dwelling remained intact. The house was derelict—its roof, doors, and windows had long since perished—and two mature trees were growing inside one of the former domestic spaces. Charmed by the trees, the architects decided to preserve them and incorporate them into the design concept. While most of the roof has been tiled following age-old traditions, the section of the roof surrounding the trees is constructed from bamboo steel slats, allowing dappled sunlight into the small, private courtyard. To compensate for the living space given over to the trees, the architects extended the adjacent rooms, creating an open, gourd-shaped courtyard at the heart of the development. A vertical bamboo grille lines the undulating curved walls of the central courtyard, and a series of bamboo steel doors open directly into the dwelling spaces. Inside, there are two self-contained apartments as well as separate spaces for exhibitions and events. The overall aesthetic of the renovated property is resolutely modern. However, the structure retains the architectural texture of the original building and, with it, the traditional vernacular concept of the historic *siheyuan*-style dwellings that typify China's inner-city residential areas. ∎

→ Skylights fill the spaces between the walls of the original building and the new bamboo skin of the courtyard.

↘ Looking beyond the tree space and into the gourd-shaped courtyard beyond.

↓ The architects designed what they call "a room in the middle of the house" to keep the trees.

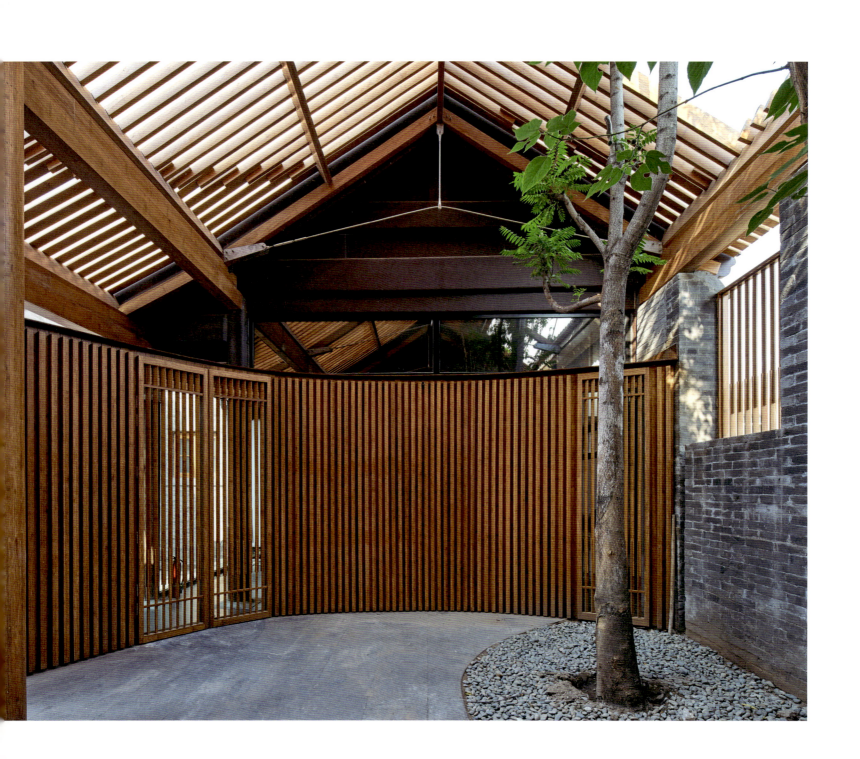

Reviving a Residential Beijing Courtyard into an Intriguing Inner-City Residence

Without altering the original structure of this typical Chinese *siheyuan*-style dwelling, Beijing-based architectural practice ARCHSTUDIO has given this traditional residence behind a battered street facade a surprising twist. This type of home is common in China's densely populated cities and typically features an enclosed central courtyard surrounded by single-story domestic volumes. Dubbing their creation Twisting Courtyard, the architects have maximized the space available by focusing on the outside space and introducing echoes of the exterior styling to the living spaces beyond, softening the boundaries between the two spaces. The principal feature is a sinuous gray brick path that winds through the courtyard and into the interiors at either end. It twists and turns up to roof height inside and outside, forging a dynamic integration of interior and exterior spaces. Curved walls neatly conceal the service areas—kitchen, bathroom, and storage spaces—from view. The airy open-plan rooms also have a special twist—they are furnished with integrated beds, tables, and curtain partitions that allow the occupants to change a room's function with ease, making them extremely versatile. Depending on what is required by visitors or guests, this *siheyuan* complex can be rented out for daytime recreation, meeting and gathering, but it can also serve as a self-contained family hostel with three bedrooms. ▌

↑ The aim of the design was to get rid of the solemn and stereotypical perception of the *siheyuan* development by creating open and active living spaces.

← The four volumes of this *siheyuan* are built from the same gray bricks that make up the "twisting" courtyard.

↓ Throughout the design, the colors are neutral—just gray, black, white, and the warm tones of natural wood.

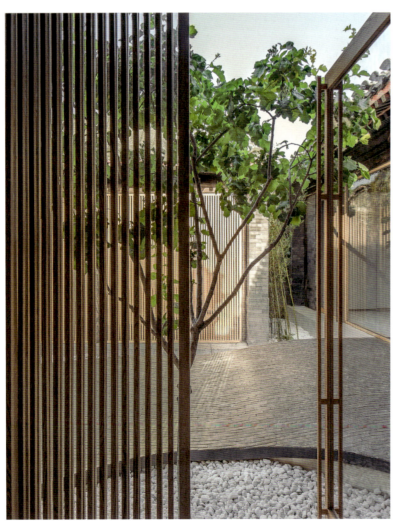

↑ The volume at the north of the development doubles as a bedroom, with a bed cleverly concealed within the wall cavity.

→ In the tatami room (see previous pages), a table rises from the center of the floor so that it can also function as a tearoom.

← A hawthorn tree in the courtyard was an original feature and has been kept to be part of the twisting landscape.

DESIGNER	anySCALE
PROJECT	Wuyuan Skywells Hotel
LOCATION	Yan Village, Wuyuan County, Jiangxi Province

A 14-Room Boutique Hotel Preserves a 300-Year-Old Huizhou-Style Mansion

Tucked away in a part of rural China seemingly untouched by modernity, Wuyuan Skywells combines the comforts of a boutique hotel with the elegance of Chinese tradition. The scheme is the work of design studio anySCALE, whose primary task was to preserve as much of the 300-year-old Huizhou-style mansion as possible. The team adopted a sensitive approach, retaining original elements in public areas while equipping 14 private guest suites with modern amenities and a more contemporary flair. A major feature of the property was its original timber frame, decorated with ornate hand carving. Many of the reliefs had suffered decades of neglect, so anySCALE enlisted local artisan Yuzong to bring them back to life. As well as restoring as many of the original designs as he could, Yuzong introduced designs of his own, based on the life story of the building's new owner. In this way, a subtle blending of old and new starts to take shape. This attention to detail can also be seen in the hotel's three "skywells" from which it takes its name. Skywells, typical in the region, are tall narrow internal courtyards that allow natural light to fill the interiors. This strategy enabled the designers to avoid altering the external appearance of the original building by adding large windows. The architects also introduced latticed panels on the facing walls and high-quality artificial lighting as part of the scheme. In the words of the hoteliers, such measures help preserve "what has been left to us by generations past, while adding our own touches for generations to come." ▮

↑ A narrow doorway leads from a serene stone courtyard into the hotel's main reception room.

→ The main entrance hall is a grand double-height space with flagstone flooring, elegant wood paneling, and a gallery lined with intricate latticework.

↓ The hotel's contemporary additions are just that—there is no apology for juxtaposing new with old and no attempt to disguise either.

← There is a sense of deep calm in the original mansion rooms, with their warm natural surfaces and rich earthy colors and textures.

↙ The hotel comprises 14 suites, each decorated with warm neutrals and wood furniture.

↓ One of the three skywells from which the hotel takes its name, with lattice windows allowing light into the rooms beyond.

↑ Yuzong's carvings are particularly noteworthy in the entrance area, where they appear on the main beams and a frieze on the reception desk front.

→ The original brick and clay walls have been restored and rebuilt according to local tradition; they keep the structure cool during hot summers.

VECTOR ARCHITECTS

A studio whose small, elegant coastal projects turned heads internationally is now in a prime position to make the most of China's growing cities.

Vector Architects, the Beijing-based studio founded by Dong Gong in 2008, has sometimes battled for the recognition it deserves. There was a danger that the small practice known for interesting but nonetheless minor projects, would be blocked from the expansive projects open to the goliath design institutes, while remaining the architects of choice for pretty, often holiday locations.

Dong graduated in architecture at the prestigious Tsinghua University before completing a master's at the University of Illinois. He then worked for several years at firms in Chicago and New York, cementing his international perspective—his easy-breezy North American delivery of English confirms this. Dong is generally humble when there is any talk of Vector Architects being at the forefront of Chinese architecture. He describes a two-tier system, with design institutes that sometimes employ over 2,000 architects dominating and small, independent outfits such as his own struggling to pick up important commissions. "Architectural design is almost becoming a production line," laments Dong pointing to the pressures of quantity and speed that have facilitated China's rapid urbanization. He concedes that, in this landscape, Vector's design stands out in comparison to so much of what is happening in the country.

Dong explains that for many years Vector, like other small studios, was left out in the cold, unable to access the large, interesting urban projects that he would have wanted to take part in. Lately, however, he believes that things are changing, and he is working on a list of →

"If only architects paid more attention to site conditions, and tried to make architecture that engages with the conditions," implores Dong Gong. "That's the only way architecture can be real."

←   The Seashore Chapel stands close to the sea, raised on concrete columns. When the tide comes in, seawater washes in beneath the building (previous pages).

→   For Captain's House, which teeters on the Huangqi Peninsula coast, the architects renovated the home with a special eye on keeping the wet, coastal conditions outdoors.

↑   To prevent water from entering the building, the architects added a vaulted roof above the third floor and built windows out beyond the structure's main frame.

↑ The Seashore Library sits directly on the sand
   in Bohai Bay, some three hours' drive from Beijing.

→ A narrow, cantilevered staircase leads up to a small
   terrace on the roof of the building.

← A meditation space has been created close to the
   reading room; slender windows facing east and west
   filter light into the space.

→   projects that are "of a good size, in a good location, and a good city." Positioning and site have always been of utmost importance for the studio—their buildings tend to be modest in scale and often occupy spectacular locations.

They have designed a series of coastal structures that have drawn much attention: the Seashore Library in Qinhuangdao Shi, the renovation of the Captain's House in Fuzhou, and perhaps most arresting of all, the Seashore Chapel, also in Qinhuangdao Shi. The location of these is more than just a consideration; it almost defines their very architectural integrity. "If only architects paid more attention to site conditions, and tried to make architecture that engages with the conditions," implores Dong. "That's the only way architecture can be real."

Despite humbly brushing off accolades, Dong is confident when praising what he sees as Vector's capacity, and indeed, proven ability when it comes to site considerations. "Each site is different, and we can find a lot of energies from the conditions," he explains. "Vector has this power; first, you have to respect [the differences of each site]. But it's not simply respecting. You have to be able to reveal and transform that power, turn that existing energy into something perceptible by humans." Dong's remarks might be understood as the spiritual capacity of architecture, so it is fitting but not coincidental that a religious building beautifully illustrates this: the Seashore Chapel, completed in 2016. The small but commanding structure is found at the end of a 98-foot-long (30-meter-long) path that takes the visitor straight out to the edge of the beach, toward the lapping waters of the sea.

The angled roof recalls a steeple, while a cantilevered space is devoted to meditation. The interior maximizes another vital ingredient for Vector Architects, that of sunlight: the curved overlapping roof is aligned with the highest point of the sun in summer, and the hidden windows are positioned in carefully crafted creases in the wall. White-washed walls accentuate all this perfectly, and in 2016 the chapel was hailed by the esteemed British monthly *Architectural Review* as "reminiscent of classic modern church design, from Ronchamp to Ando's Church of the Light." It's hard to disagree with what they called the building's "simple, rarified atmosphere," which applies to the exterior as much as the interior. →

↑   Inside the vast reading room of the Seashore Library,
    the seating is terraced to offer all users an
    unobstructed view of the sea.

←   The triple-height space features a soaring wall of glass,
    with sliding-glass doors that open directly onto the
    beach, plate glass windows, and a top layer of glass
    blocks that filter a more diffuse light.

"Architectural design is almost becoming a production line," laments Dong Gong pointing to the pressures of quantity and speed that have facilitated China's rapid urbanization.

↑   At the Alila Yangshuo Hotel, Vector Architects preserved an old sugar mill out, respecting the area's industrial heritage.

→   The rigid geometric volumes of the hotel mark a stark contrast with the rugged forms of the karst landscape.

Dong Gong explains that the built environment in China is so prone to change that often an architect cannot be sure what the site conditions will be just two years into the future.

→ The chapel and another of Vector's projects, the Alila Yangshuo Hotel, with its brooding mountain setting and elegant concrete structure, are masterclasses in extrapolating the surrounding landscape and interpreting it for the benefit of the visitor. Dong acknowledges that with so many visually pleasing backdrops, the studio was in danger of becoming pigeonholed as the "oceanfront guys." Given the similarities between many of his projects, the architect muses: "This is somehow the naive, funny part of the market." He considers a clientele not always well-versed in architecture, surmising that the impressive landscapes of their previous projects probably attract people who want something similar. Not wanting to seem ungrateful, Dong insists, "We appreciate this kind of fortune because we have more projects surrounded by fantastic landscapes."

However, Dong is also keen to express a more philosophical and intellectual perspective on the work of Vector Architects; being categorized as the architect who only does buildings with "pretty backdrops" would not be satisfactory for him. "I am interested in both urban and natural," he says, still on the subject of location, "but what I'm really interested in, is that the site is real," Dong explains that the built environment in China is so prone to change that often an architect cannot be sure what the site conditions will be just two years into the future. "With that kind of site, I don't feel comfortable designing because I don't have a target. I am more interested in a site with lasting conditions." →

← At the heart of the Alila Yangshuo development,
a sunken plaza and reflecting pond highlight the
significance of the old structure.

↑ The architects combined solid and hollow concrete
blocks in perforated walls that allow natural light
and ventilation to penetrate the buildings.

↓ Public walkways throughout the hotel complex offer
visitors framed views of the surrounding landscape.

→   At the Changjiang Art Museum in the Shanxi Province, completed in 2019, Vector has proven that they are also adept at building in a stable, urban environment too. The comfortingly solid curves (again reminiscent of modernist European design) are designed impressively to interact with the hastily built apartments surrounding it, and the museum contributes to a new community landscape of Vector's own making. "Many people think that architecture is a product to, let's say, represent their wealth," comments Dong when asked what he thinks the role of the architect is in China today; he adds, "I think we are in a kind of transition moment, and we need some architects to educate, or at least influence society." As cities and landscapes in China begin to stabilize, from a period of unprecedented change to an era of maturity, Vector Architects are ready and waiting to contribute by way of an altogether more well-positioned, more beautiful architectural reality.

Location and scale aside, when Dong is asked if he and his team have a guiding principle when it comes to architectural design, his answer is characteristically balanced and self-effacing: "We have a very simple rule here—all we are trying to do is good architecture." That, surely, is easier said than done, but in the years since it was established, Vector has gradually built a reputation for doing precisely that. With a clutch of astounding projects, the practice is now in a very select group of Chinese studios that have turned heads among architecture critics internationally as well as at home. ▮

↑   The Changjiang Museum stands on the edge of an urban center, facing a newly constructed residential neighborhood; resembling a solid block of red brick, it seeks to forge a link between the two.

→   At the southwest corner of the building, an outdoor staircase climbs up through the museum to a second-floor terrace open to the public.

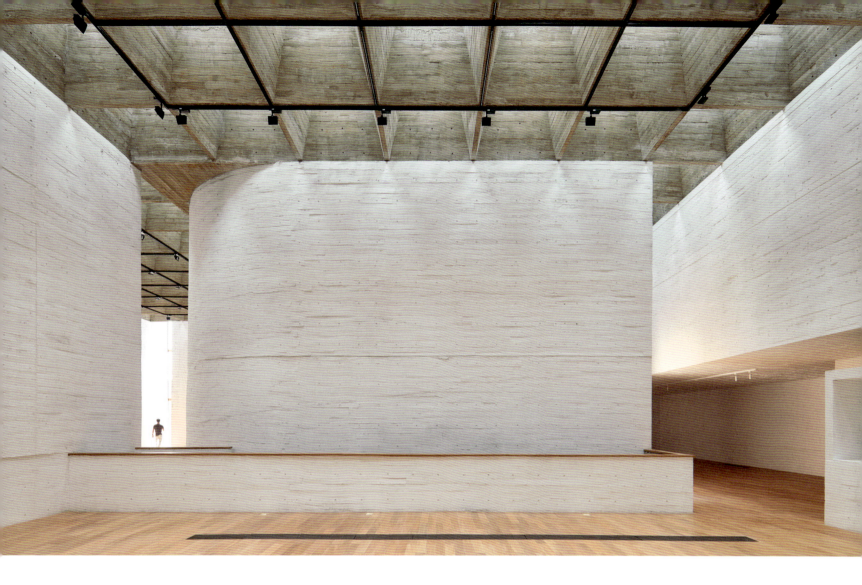

↑ Inside the galleries, natural light enters the rooms via skylights and is softened as it filters through a waffle-beam grid.

← The raised terrace on the second floor of the gallery has a tree-filled courtyard at its center and is open to the sky.

→ The galleries of the museum are arranged around a 54-foot (16-meter) light well, which is punched with windows at different levels.

↑ Open to the public and independent of the museum, the raised terrace on the second floor connects to the northern community across the street via a footbridge.

→ The same red brick has been used for all of the walls inside and out. Inside the museum, while the public spaces remain bare brick, the brickwork in the galleries has been painted white (see previous pages).

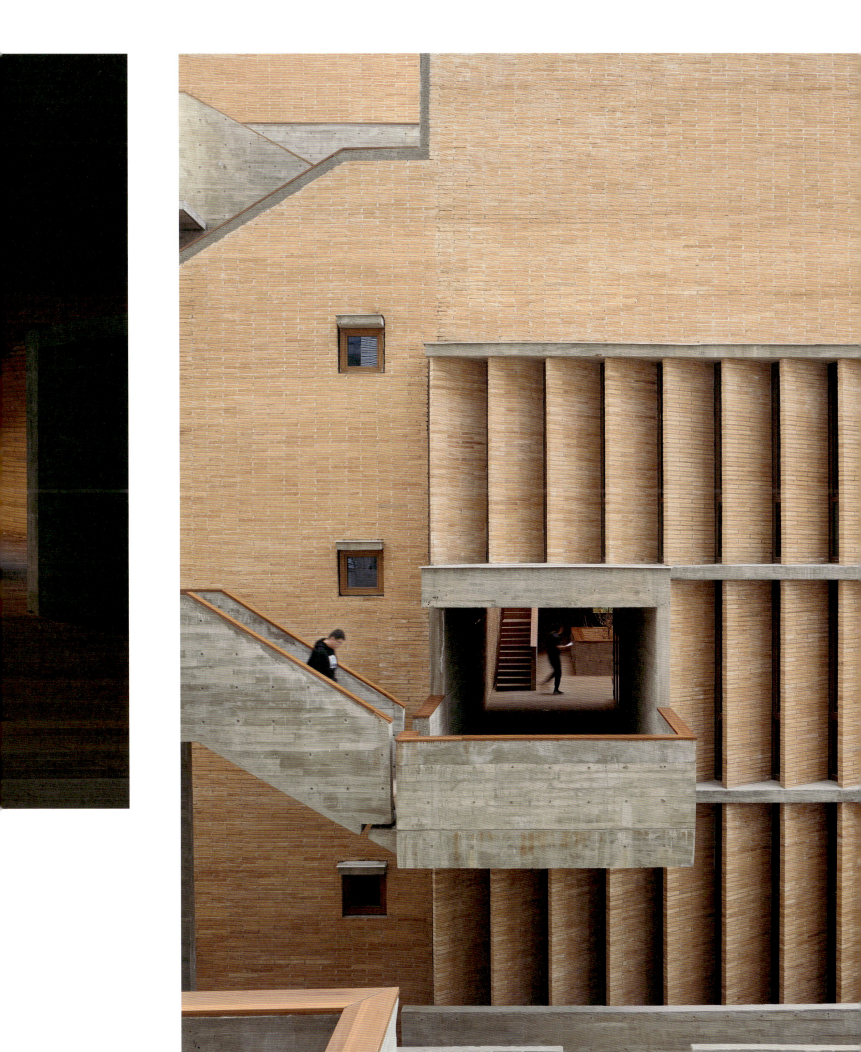

AS THOUSANDS OF NEW MUSEUMS ARE BUILT IN CHINA, ARCHITECTS COMPETE TO MAKE THEIR MARK

From 349 museums in 1978 to more than 5,000 four decades later, China's cultural building boom has produced both vanity projects and masterpieces alike.

If you travel southwest from the Bund in Shanghai, the colonial architecture lining the city's iconic waterfront gradually gives way to residential complexes, and beyond that, you'll soon find yourself in a newly developed area. There, along a several-mile stretch of Longteng Avenue, there is an impressive cluster of more than 15 museums, art centers, and galleries—a grand spectacle that perhaps only the Museumsinsel in Berlin or Amsterdam's Museumkwartier can rival. At the weekend, this area, known as West Bund, is usually packed with museum-goers and local residents jogging by the river. It may seem difficult to believe, but almost all of the structures in this world-class cultural hub were abandoned factories or empty fields only a few years ago.

The impressive West Bund cultural district is merely one recent example—though certainly one of the finest—of China's museum boom over the last two decades. In 2002, following China's successful bid for the 2008 Beijing Olympics, the State Administration of Cultural Heritage announced their intention to open 1,000 new museums across the country by 2015— a number they surpassed by 500, two years ahead of the designated deadline. Today, the country boasts over 5,100 museums, up from just 349 in 1978—the year that marked the beginning of China's economic reform and reopening to foreign influence, including Western architectural styles. In 1982, with the completion of the Fragrant Hill Hotel in Beijing, the late Chinese-American architect I. M. Pei became the first foreigner to build in China since the end of the Cultural Revolution; two decades later, Pei would again garner critical acclaim for his work on Suzhou Museum. China's eagerness to erect museums is a testament to the unparalleled symbolic status of cultural architecture amid the county's rapid urbanization

↑　The site for the Long Museum West Bund was once a coal dock.

←　The exhibitions at the Long Museum West Bund have become an important part of the cultural life of Shanghai.

and global ascent. As a vessel for the artifacts of history and civilization, contemporary museums are akin to the temples or shrines of ancient times, symbolic of a nation's status and the soft power it wields internationally. Such proliferation is also a clear acknowledgment by both the government and →

In 2008, Wang Shu and Lu Wenyu completed their masterpiece, the Ningbo Historic Museum.

The main structure of the Ningbo Historic Museum is made of steel and reinforced concrete.

→ private developers of the public's increasing appetite for art and culture, as a result of the country's economic growth. For architects, this means that a museum commission in China is one of the highest honors, with the guarantee of global visibility and, theoretically, a place in history.

Despite the broad range of aesthetic and architectural styles, most of these new cultural landmarks share a propensity for imposing scale and grandeur, just as museums tend to in the West. The striking similarities in architectural approach are unsurprising, given that architects of international note designed many of these new structures. In the early days of the boom, China had already welcomed a succession of "starchitects," including Rem Koolhaas (Times Museum in Guangzhou), Steven Holl (Sifang Art Museum in Nanjing), and David Chipperfield (Rockbund Art Museum in Shanghai), to name just a few. Today, global starchitects remain competitive in China's museum sector. M+, a public museum of visual culture designed by Swiss architects Herzog & de Meuron—the practice

behind the Tai Kwun Centre for Heritage and Art, another major Hong Kong institution which opened its doors in 2018—is currently under construction in Hong Kong's West Kowloon Cultural District. It is expected to be one of the highest-caliber art museums in the world, on par with the Museum of Modern Art in New York and Tate Modern in London.

Meanwhile, on the mainland, homegrown architects have caught up in recent years. Besides the widely acclaimed Ningbo Museum, designed by Wang Shu, and the Ordos Museum, designed by Ma Yansong's MAD Architects, another prominent example is Long Museum West Bund, by Shanghai-based practice Atelier Deshaus. From the outset, this was a high-profile project, mostly due to the immense wealth of owners Liu Yiqian and Wang Wei, a billionaire couple whose world-renowned collection, ranging from antiques to contemporary art, includes, among other things, Amedeo Modigliani's Reclining Nude, which Liu purchased for $170.4 million (about €130 million) back in 2015. The design of Long Museum West Bund certainly matches its owners' extravagance: Atelier Deshaus's Liu Yichun and Chen Yifeng preserved a 328-foot-long (100-meter-long) coal-hopper unloading bridge at the center of the site, which was formerly a wharf, and it is surrounded by various gallery spaces in a series of umbrella-like vaulted concrete volumes oriented in different directions. They penetrate the existing underground two-story parking garage, successfully repurposing it as the four-story museum's basement. Windows shaded by fixed metal louvers built into some of the arched ceilings bathe the gallery space with daylight and illuminate the works on display. The transformation of the dilapidated industrial buildings has created an awe-inspiring masterpiece.

While urban metropolises like Shanghai boast museums that are majestic in scale, rural China has welcomed a plethora of new buildings that are more remarkable for their conceptual ingenuity. Completed in 2018 in the Aranya Gold Coast →

→ Hong Kong's M+, designed by Herzog & de Meuron, is a cultural center for 20th- and 21st-century art, design, architecture, and moving image.

↑ The facade of the Ningbo Historic Museum is made of a wide range of recycled bricks and tiles.

China's eagerness to erect museums is a testament to the
unparalleled symbolic status of cultural architecture amid
the county's rapid urbanization and global ascent.

For architects, this means that a museum commission in China is one of the highest honors with the guarantee of global visibility and, theoretically, a place in history.

On a beach along the coast of northern China's Bohai Bay, the UCCA Dune Art Museum is carved into the sand.

→ Community of Beidaihe District in Hebei Province, the UCCA Dune Museum—designed by Li Hu and Huang Wenjing of OPEN Architecture—is the culmination of a partnership between resort developer Aranya and the UCCA Foundation (whose flagship museum, UCCA Center for Contemporary Art, sits at the center of the 798 Art District in Beijing, and was renovated under the direction of OMA). Winner of the 2017 Iconic Awards Best of Best, the 107,640-square-foot (10,000-square-meter) museum is composed of ten interconnected galleries, seven of which are indoor and carved into the surrounding sand dune, meaning that the building blends seamlessly into its natural surroundings. Apertures carved into the walls of the ground-floor galleries and a viewing platform on the roof of the building offer visitors spectacular views of the Bohai Sea. As a non-collecting museum, the ecologically attuned architecture sets the tone for future exhibition programs, which will focus on connecting humans and nature through art.

With thousands of new museums mushrooming across China in just two decades, one has to wonder about the quality of the collections displayed inside them, and whether they are equipped with sufficient "software"—trained staff, ethical management—to keep them in operation. Recently, there have been alarming reports of ghost museums that stand in quiet solitude after their grand openings. Many of them were built by private developers less out of a genuine passion for art and culture than as leeway for governmental approval to appropriate public land for their ambitious construction projects, so the lack of professionalism and similarly wanting

rigor in programming is only to be expected. This situation leads to a question about the ethics of architecture: as China moves towards a post-boom era, is it enough for museums to have a gorgeous facade if they provide no other public service?

Architects are certainly divided on these issues. Speaking at a conference on China's "museumification" in 2016, Steven Holl argued for architects' right to design museums even in the absence of clients or adequate programming, asserting that "architecture, in and of itself, is a force." Others call for architecture to play a more active role in engaging audiences and local ecosystems around the site. As OPEN Architecture's Li Hu observed in an interview, while architects may not be able to change the situation, they can "at least choose the right one to work on and make an authentic contribution to public culture." Whichever side you're on, the fact is that amid China's recent proliferation of museums, it is still rare for their architecture and content to complement one another harmoniously—but when they do, like in I. M. Pei's design for Suzhou Museum, the result is an incomparable achievement. The Suzhou Museum impeccably fuses elements from local vernacular architecture—dark-gray clay tile roofs, white plaster walls, and, most crucially, unity between building and garden—with Pei's signature modernist sensibility, characterized by the ubiquitous play of geometric folds. Pei's masterful blend of tradition and modern finesse resonates powerfully with the collection of ancient Chinese art, calligraphy, and crafts housed within. Unlike the imposing structures of so many museums being built today, the Suzhou Museum sits humbly in the city's historic quarter, appearing to be an extension of it. There is certainly hope that the architects behind the museums of the future will learn from the greatest examples of the past. ▮

I. M. Pei's design for the Suzhou Museum combines traditional architectural principles with modern elements.

DESIGNER	OPEN Architecture
PROJECT	UCCA Dune Art Museum
LOCATION	Bohai Bay, Qinhuangdao, Hebei Province

Striking a Delicate Balance between Nature and Architecture

On a quiet beach along the coast of northern China's Bohai Bay, curious protrusions emerge from the sand dunes. They belong to the UCCA Dune Art Museum, which lies beneath the surface and comprises a series of curvaceous interconnected spaces that resemble caves. It seems appropriate that visitors to the gallery are invited to appreciate art in the most primal and timeless form of space, as they are reminiscent of humankind's earliest "art galleries." The decision to build this subterranean art museum arose from Beijing-based OPEN Architecture's desire to protect the delicate local dune ecosystem, which has evolved over many thousands of years. According to the architects, the siting of the museum will ensure that the sand dunes will be preserved "instead of being leveled to make space for ocean-view real estate developments, as has happened to many other dunes along the shore." The cavernous spaces include eight interlinked galleries and a cafe. Construction workers in the port city of Qinhuangdao hand-crafted the rounded concrete shells that make up the museum's structure using formwork molds made primarily from small strips of wood. The architects deliberately retained the irregular and imperfect texture left by the formwork, allowing visitors to see traces of the building's manual construction. And the protrusions? These are funnels and openings that allow natural light to fill the museum's spaces. They also frame different views of the outside world so that museum visitors can observe and appreciate ever-changing views of the sky and the sea throughout the day. ▌

↑ A doorway leads from the main foyer and directly onto the beach beyond.

← Seen from above, the museum resembles a curious collection of organic forms.

→ Pools of light stream into the cavernous rooms via the funnels that rise up into the landscape.

↑ Elements of the building continue beyond its boundaries, blurring the lines between inside and outside space.

→ Inside the gallery, the soft, hand-molded walls create a cocoon-like atmosphere.

DESIGNER	Atelier FCJZ
PROJECT	Jishou Art Museum
LOCATION	Jishou, Xiangxi, Hunan Province

A Bridge That Gives City Dwellers a Chance to Appreciate Art while Crossing the River

In this original interpretation of a traditional style of bridge, architectural firm Atelier FCJZ has designed a home for an art museum in the city of Jishou in Hunan Province that spans the Wanrong River. Instead of building the museum in an out-of-town location, as was originally intended, the architects suggested that it should be located in the city center. The design comprises two bridges spanning the river: on the lower level, an open steel-truss structure provides a covered pedestrian river crossing; and up above are the glass facades of the museum, which features a long corridor that serves as the main hall for temporary exhibitions. Visitors can access the museum from either end of the bridge via supplementary spaces that include an entrance hall, an administrative office, a shop, and a tearoom. This form of bridge is known as *fengyu qiao* in Chinese, which translates as "wind-and-rain bridge." Characteristic of this mountainous region of China, the design allows pedestrians to while away some time while sheltering from bad weather. FCJZ applied this concept to the Jishou Art Museum, intending to make art accessible to all, so that "people in Jishou would not only make a special trip to see art but will also encounter art on their way to work, to school, or to shop." ▎

↑   Above the steel pedestrian walkway sits the museum's glass and concrete structure.

←   On both riverbanks, the front entrances of the museum are fully integrated within the mixed-use facade of the city street.

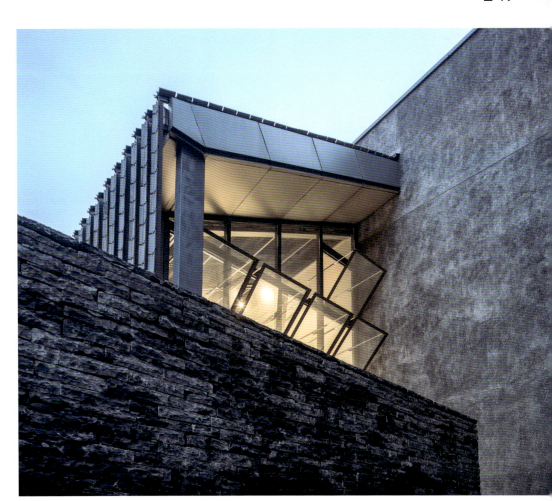

↑ Glass walls enclose the exhibition area, entrance, and exit.

← At the entrance to the Great Exhibition Hall, a flight of stairs leads up to the painting gallery within the concrete bridge.

↓ Looking along the length of the Great Exhibition Hall, with the concrete bridge above.

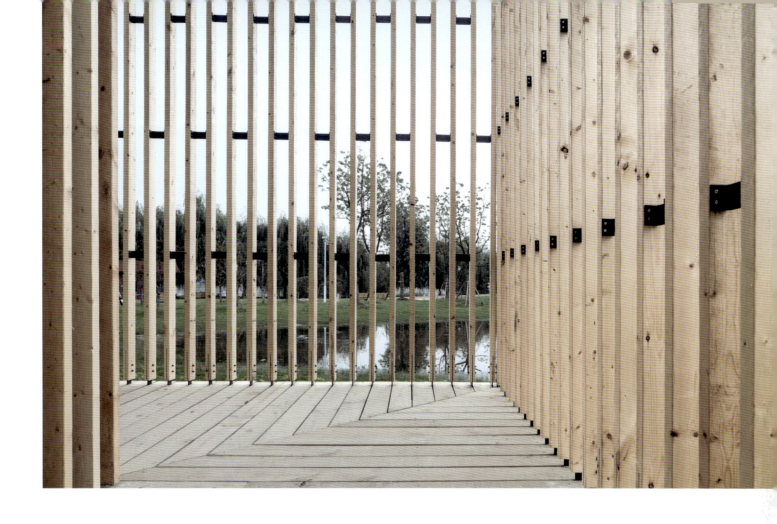

AZL ARCHITECTS

With a scholarly approach, AZL has carefully contributed to regional architecture where materials and community take center stage.

In many ways, AZL (Atelier Zhang Lei), a studio founded by Zhang Lei in Nanjing back in 2001, is a forerunner of the small-scale architecture practices that have proliferated in China in recent years. Zhang began his career in the academic world of design institutes that dominate the sector in China, but desiring change, he decided to leave teaching and research behind and "launch into the practice part," he recalls sitting at his desk. However, research remains an essential element of AZL's work, only now, very much within the context of architectural practice. Their projects are underpinned by detailed analysis of regional building traditions with a mission to redefine the relationship between built and natural environments.

   When observing nearly two decades of development it's easy to be struck at the sheer scale of change that has defined China's built environment. The level of change in architecture, in terms of education and practice, comes as no surprise, but as Zhang describes the recent past, there is a wistful tone in his voice, suggesting that he finds it difficult even to recall the time in question. There has been a significant increase in access to the architecture profession, and Zhang points out that in 2001 there were only about 20 to 30 architecture schools in China—now the figure is closer to 300. However, Zhang feels a sense of nostalgia for a time when the sector was much less regulated. "I preferred the working environment and conditions back →

"Local materials and local craftsmanship are also essential," says
Zhang Lei. "These choices make a pleasant, better environment
for users. With the right building materials, we can create
a robust link between architecture and the environment."

↑   Nanjing Wanjing Garden Chapel. A wood-strip facade
    forms a double shell around the central hall, flooding
    internal corridors with light.

→   Inside the chapel itself, the brilliant white surfaces—
    pews, walls, floors, and ceiling—emphasize the spiritual
    experience for worshippers.

→   then," he says before beginning a lament that architects all over the world are familiar with: building codes that regulate all aspects of AZL's projects, and Zhang seems to think much of it is too onerous.

Increasingly strict building codes and planning regulations haven't prevented AZL from building an impressive portfolio of projects, each with an integral connection to their surroundings, function, and community. Two of their recent buildings, the Nanjing Wanjing Garden Chapel and the Shitang Internet Conference Center, appear to be radically different, but they both demonstrate a pragmatic yet refined sensibility that is achieved through the thoughtful selection of construction materials and careful consideration of the local context. They were also both built in an exceptionally short space of time—around 45 days each. Zhang explains that with both projects they "wanted to create a public space rather than an iconic image. Moreover, we didn't have time to create an iconic image."

In a trait that can be seen in much of their work, AZL tends to invest much of their efforts in establishing relationships between people and the environment. According to Zhang this is grounded in traditional Chinese culture, where much importance is placed on the notion of uniting heaven (the environment) and earth (people). AZL is merely providing the meeting place for this union. At Nanjing Wanjing Chapel, exposed rafters draw the eye (and hopefully the soul) toward the ceiling where light floods in, emphasizing the height of the space. Views of the landscape surrounding the chapel are filtered by the semi-open external shell of timber panels. Although it is on a far larger and more industrial scale, wood and the inclusion of the surrounding landscape are also fundamental to AZL's design for Shitang Internet Conference Center. "Local materials and local craftsmanship are also essential," continues Zhang.   →

→   At the Shitang Internet Conference Center an oversized roof is raised on a series of slender columns to provide a canopy for shelter.

↘   Almost the entire facade is made from strips of timber.

↓   The building borrows typologies from existing Chinese forms, notably large commune auditoriums and greenhouses.

Increasingly strict building codes and planning regulations haven't prevented AZL from building an impressive portfolio of projects, each with an integral connection to their surroundings, function, and community.

↑   In Song House, AZL introduced an atrium to a family home, a modern interpretation of the traditional internal courtyard, surrounded by the five bedrooms of the home's residents.

→   Although Song House mirrors the scale and basic language of its neighbor, it makes a dramatic addition to the street with its quirky white facade.

↑   The BingDing Wood Kiln. Arched windows above the second
    floor of the building are filled with lattices of kiln bricks that
    cast light into the interior.

→   The ground floor houses a vast space for daily work such as
    glazing, molding, polishing, enameling, and porcelain storage.

→ "These choices make a pleasant, better environment for users. With the right building materials, we can create a robust link between architecture and the environment."

AZL's approach to materiality, combined with a deep social and cultural impetus, gives their projects a recognizable and well-defined identity. They are at once simple and complex: the Nanjing Wanjing Chapel was erected rapidly from inexpensive materials, but the intricate and exacting application of these materials evokes a profound spatial experience. Similarly, at another of AZL's recent projects, the BingDing Wood Kiln near Jingdezhen, the traditional center of porcelain production in China, the studio's cultural vision is clear. The design of the structure, created as a ceremonial space intended to inspire workers and visitors alike, exhibits a clear architectural reverence to the traditional craft performed here, accentuated by the simple construction materials chosen (concrete for the main structure and brick for the egg-shaped kiln itself). The factory nestles into the bamboo-covered mountainous landscape surrounding it, illustrating the union of people and the environment that Zhang is keen to point out. The serenity and architectural integrity of what is essentially an industrial space also speak to AZL's commitment to building on the knowledge of rural crafts and traditions.

Zhang explains that he spent four years working on three rural projects near Hangzhou: "I visited the area more than 200 times, I think," he says in a diligent rather than boastful manner. When asked what he thinks the role of the architect is in China today, his response is unequivocal: the architect's role is to "extend the boundary of human civilization." He concludes, "It's what I would call an open attitude to the public." Zhang, like the buildings he and his team design, is complex; he is keen to add that, in his opinion, people talk about culture and context too much in China. "I don't want to make a label for myself as a *Chinese architect* or something like that." That would be far too simplistic. The word *vanguard* has been often used when describing Zhang and AZL, and one wonders if he likes this accolade. Ever the contrarian, he simply replies, "No, no, I am the *real* guard," and laughs. ▌

AZL's projects are underpinned by detailed analysis of regional building traditions with a mission to redefine the relationship between built and natural environments.

In a trait that can be seen in much of their work, AZL tends to invest much of their efforts in establishing relationships between people and the environment.

DESIGNER	Atelier Deshaus
PROJECT	Long Museum West Bund
LOCATION	Shanghai

Bridging the Gap between Contemporary Urban Architecture and the Industrial Age

The Long Museum West Bund plays a significant role in the cultural life of Shanghai, drawing art lovers to exhibitions from a diverse range of artists, including James Turrell, Antony Gormley, Olafur Eliasson, Louise Bourgeois, Xu Zhen, and Xiang Jing (see p. 267), among others. However, visitors do not come purely for the art—they also come to see the landmark galleries in which the exhibitions are displayed. Located on Huangpu River in the Xuhui District of Shanghai, this museum occupies land formerly used as a wharf for bringing coal into the city. Repurposing an industrial site to serve as a state-of-the-art cultural hub is not unique, but this particular example, designed by Shanghai-based Atelier Deshaus, is unusual because the entire complex is oriented around the wharf's dilapidated coal-hopper unloading bridge. A row of disused coal hoppers run through the center of the hulking concrete volume measuring 360 feet (110 meters) long, 33 feet (10 meters) wide, and 26 feet (8 meters) high. Flanking this structure along its entire length are two contemporary buildings that arch toward each other above the bridge, enveloping the structure beneath their outsweeping walls. This "umbrella" vaulting is also a significant feature inside the gallery, where it creates large, free-form interiors. Oriented in different directions, some of the vaults stretch right up to the roof, while others frame exhibition spaces, as one room flows seamlessly into the next. ▌

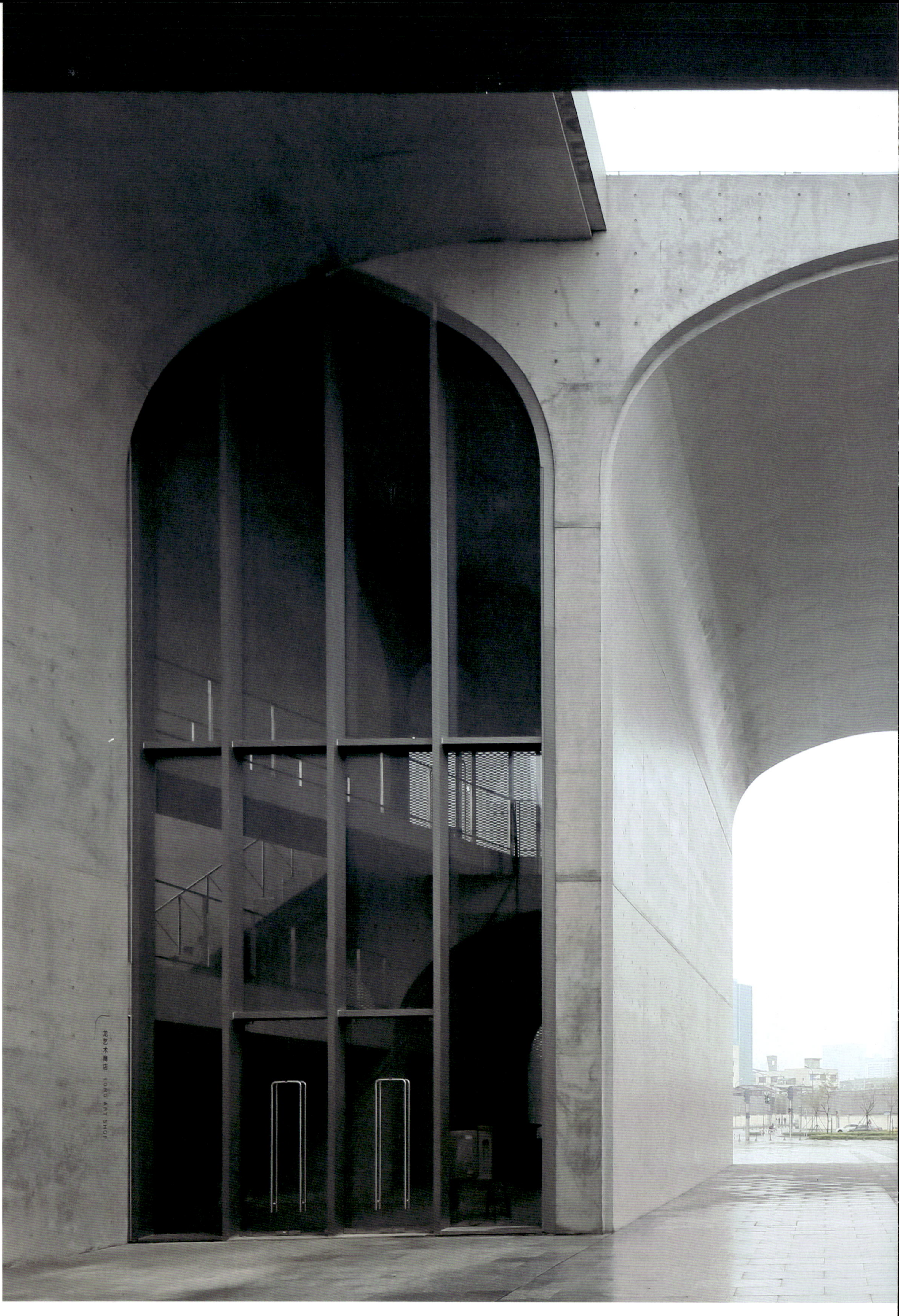
LONG ART SHOP

A Buddhist Shrine Infused with the Words of its Spiritual Leader

The Water-Moon Monastery rises from the vast Guandu Plain north of Taipei City on Taiwan's northern tip. Standing serenely in front of a 262-foot-long (80-meter-long) lotus pond with the verdant slopes of Datun Mountain behind it, the shrine and its surroundings exude tranquility. A spiritual center for the Dharma Drum Buddhist Group, the monastery was named by its founder, Master Sheng Yen, whose vision of the site was as a "flower in space, moon in water." KRIS YAO | ARTECH's interpretation of Sheng Yen's vision involved making the lower part of the shrine transparent so that the upper portion appears to "float" gracefully in mid-air. The design is minimal, and aside from the upper section, which is clad in wood, the primary construction material is concrete. The monastery, reflected in the lotus pond's still waters, is fronted with massive columns with flowing golden drapes suspended between them. The Chinese characters of the *Diamond Sutra* perforate the concrete panels, imbuing them with spiritual meaning and allowing sunlight to filter through. On the west side of the shrine, a massive wooden wall is carved with the Chinese characters of the famous *Heart Sutra*. As sunlight shines through the characters, they are projected onto the surfaces within the building, imprinting columns, walls, and even the inhabitants, with the wise words of Buddha's teaching. ▮

DESIGNER	KRIS YAO | ARTECH
PROJECT	Water-Moon Monastery
LOCATION	Taipei, Taiwan

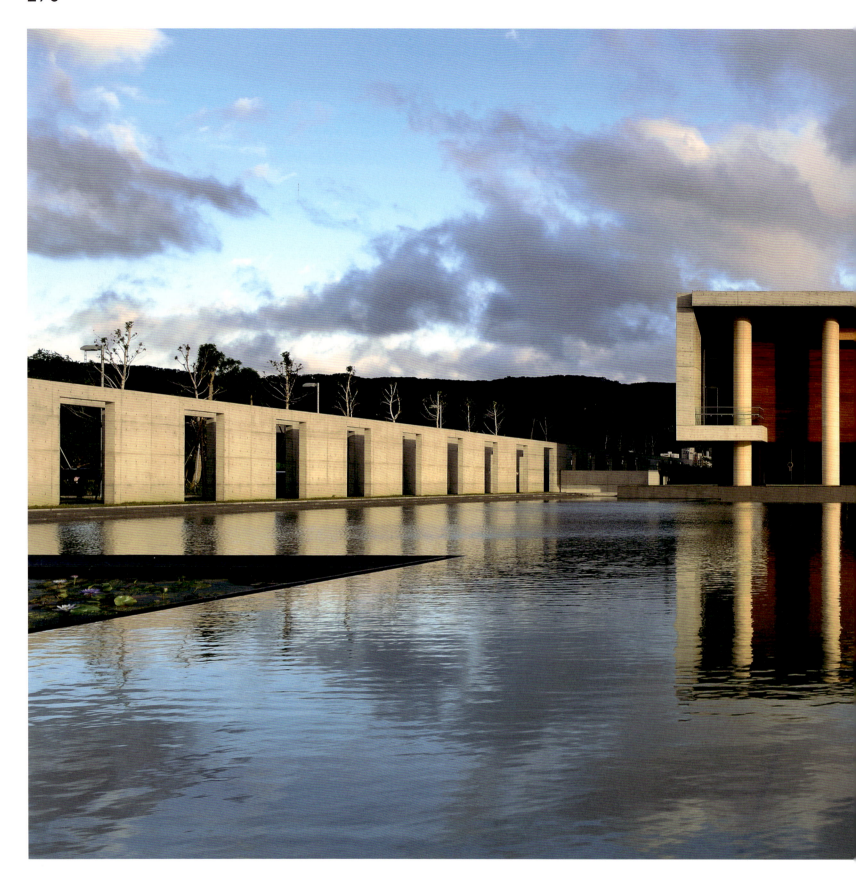

The contemporary design marks a considerable departure from traditional Chinese monastery architecture.

↑   Two walls of different heights serve as a buffer from the expressway beyond the site.

→   Sun-blessed Chinese characters line the columns beyond the inscription carved into the wall.

←   The carved panels in the facade are not only decorative, but help shield the interior from direct sunlight.

DESIGNER	Waterfrom Design
PROJECT	TEA Community Center
LOCATION	Xiamen

A New Interpretation of Tradition in Search of Tranquility

Architecture studio Waterfrom Design took inspiration from Chinese tradition to design a multi-use space that will serve the local community in the long term. Elements of their design symbolize the harmony and simplicity of rural village life, and the ancient Chinese fable, *The Peach Blossom Spring*, provided an additional reference point. They embraced an age-old cultural pastime by dedicating the top floor of the building to drinking tea: at street level, there is a window-lined tea pavilion surrounded by a square-shaped body of water, and below it, there is a series of versatile rooms that can be used for dining, reading, lectures, and exhibitions. Sunlight, air, and water are themes that are repeated throughout the center in a variety of inventive ways. For example, inside the tea pavilion, water flows along a channel in the long communal table before passing through the glass wall into the pool of water outside. A narrow staircase leads down to the level below, and visitors are momentarily cast into cool darkness as they descend before emerging once more into another bright and airy space. An ever-changing pattern of shadows and reflections from the pool above dance along the walls, imbuing the rooms with a tranquil meditative atmosphere. At the center of the building is a circular glass-enclosed courtyard with a mature tree growing in the middle—symbolizing the tradition of village gatherings and storytelling under trees. The material palette is simple, neutral, and natural—soft limestone, dull copper, handmade pottery, fragrant fir wood, and woven rattan. The rhythm of life is slow, and the atmosphere quiet. ∎

↑ An overwhelming sense of peace and tranquility pervades all of the rooms, thanks to the sparse furnishings and natural tones.

← The tree casts shadows into the lower-ground spaces, creating an almost dreamy atmosphere for people gathering here.

→ Light reflects from the pool of water outside to cast rippled shadows on the ceiling of the tearoom.

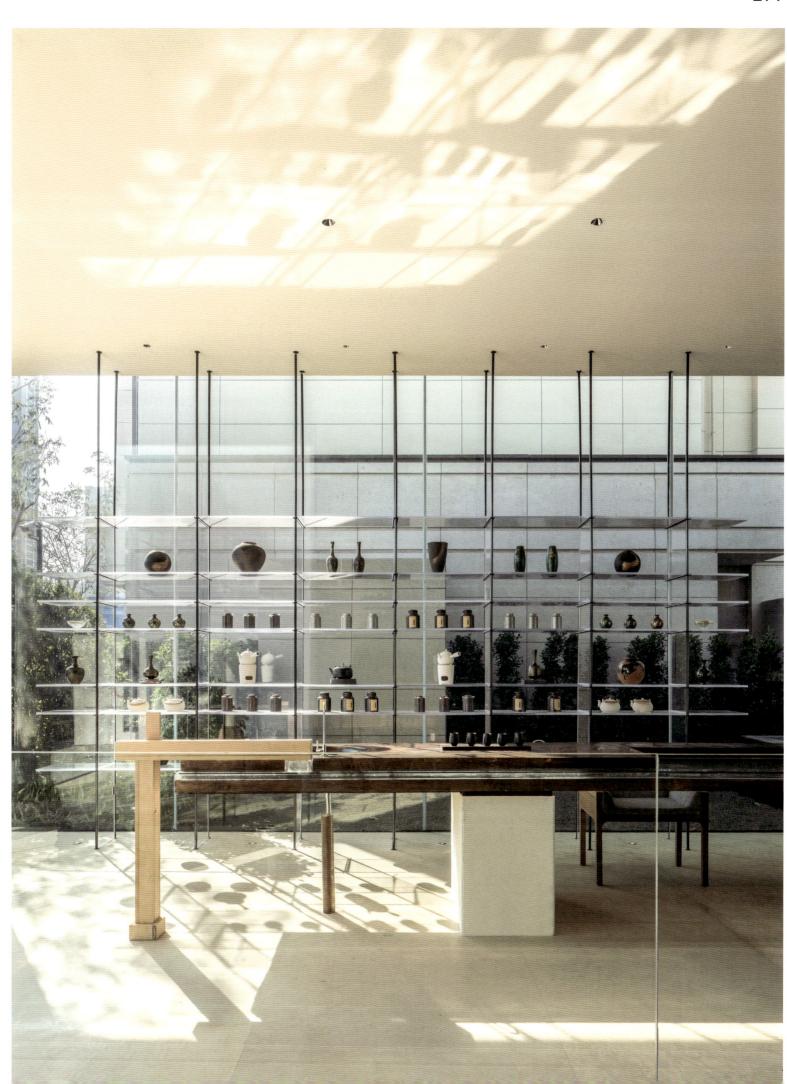

The ceiling appears to float above the room with a halo of light streaming in from the floor above.

DESIGNER	O-office Architects
PROJECT	Lianzhou Museum of Photography
LOCATION	Lianzhou, Guangdong Province

A Museum Dedicated to Photography Combines Old and Contemporary Aesthetics

Occupying the site of a disused sugar mill in the heart of Lianzhou's old city center, the Lianzhou Museum of Photography is the culmination of a series of photography festivals held annually on the site for more than a decade. In keeping with the art form, which can be avant-garde and provocative, the state-of-the-art design for the building combines modern architecture with reclaimed materials. Designed by O-office Architects, the building is one of two parts inter-connected with open hallways and staircases: a preexisting three-story warehouse, which now houses the permanent exhibition halls, enclosed by a new, U-shaped building with transparent walls. This part of the complex is suspended above ground level to create fluid open spaces for public events below, including four further exhibition halls, a library, a conference hall, and offices. Outdoor spaces connect the street to the front of the building and the alley at the rear, establishing the museum as an organic part of the neighborhood. Above, a folded canopy shelters visitors from the elements. The extension was constructed using old pottery tiles, bricks, and wooden window frames salvaged from the original buildings. The combination of the old and the new gives the building a sense of history, but also continuity, and represents a respectful approach to the regeneration of the city's historical center. ▌

↑ The new structure wraps around the original building, with external stairs connecting the levels.

← Nestled into the V-shaped roof is a series of steps intended for use as a theater.

↓ A diffuse light permeates the interior spaces through the semitransparent walls.

DESIGNER	Amateur Architecture Studio
PROJECT	Ningbo Historic Museum
LOCATION	Ningbo

A Legacy-Defining Museum Made with Reclaimed Materials

Just to the north of Yinzhou Park in the city of Ningbo, the Ningbo Historic Museum occupies space in a massive plaza landscaped with fountains and newly planted trees. Inspired by a mountain landscape rather than the urban one it serves, the three-story building is an enormous hulking form with impressive outward-sloping walls. The mountain motif is emphasized by a number of courtyards at various levels within the complex, which can be interpreted as valleys, crevices, and caves. The random placement and varied size of the windows add to the effect. The creation of Wang Shu and Lu Wenyu, the founders of Amateur Architecture Studio, the museum exemplifies the studio's approach to architecture. Despite its resolutely contemporary design, the building utilizes waste material from local demolitions. Rather than contribute to the ever-growing number of anonymous steel-and-glass structures of the modern age, it is Amateur Architecture Studio's desire to forge a link with history and tradition in their designs, often in the fabric of the buildings themselves. Here, for example, the facades incorporate irregular patches of old terra-cotta and clay tiles and rough gray stone. It was just such an approach that earned the practice's co-founder Wang Shu praise from the Pritzker Architecture Prize jury in their search for designs that anchor works in tradition while looking firmly toward the future. ∎

← Random geometric openings in the facade are a characteristic feature of the practice's designs.

↙ The architects used bamboo molds to cast concrete sections of the wall inside and out.

↓ The facades incorporate recycled bricks and tiles from around 30 villages demolished in the area. Some of the materials date back over a thousand years.

NERI&HU

A husband-and-wife duo achieves synchronicity between architectural, interior, furniture, and even graphic design.

"Contrary to what many people think: that we are extremely strategic, that we have this innate sense of what is going to happen, none of that is true!" exclaims Lyndon Neri as he cozily sits beside his wife and business partner Rossana Hu on the couch. They founded Neri&Hu in 2004 in Shanghai and are now among the most sought-after architecture and design studios in the city, if not in all of China. But despite Neri's gushing, vivacious, and ultimately very confident demeanor, he insists that, far from being some genius act of "brilliance," setting up in China and managing to capitalize on an explosion in demand and their own unique cultural identity was merely circumstantial.

While Neri was overseeing projects for his then-employer, the office of famed postmodernist New York architect Michael Graves, they found themselves stuck in China due to the SARS epidemic and then decided not to return to the United States, where they had begun their careers as architects. Rather than having some sort of foresight or knowing what the future would hold, the young couple was concerned that their children should not lose their grounding in the family's Chinese roots. Whether intentionally business savvy or not, that decision proved to be the right one. →

→ At the Tsingpu Yangzhou Retreat, Neri&Hu were tasked with integrating several existing buildings in a landscape dotted with small lakes into a luxury twenty-room hotel.

↘ The architects unified the disparate elements by laying a grid of walls and paths across the site, creating a number of courtyard enclosures.

↓ Inside the hotel, a continuation of the brick walls and paths is married with dark, glossy wood accents to create an overlap between interior and exterior.

↑ At the Aranya Art Center, a public space beneath the central void often functions as a water feature, but can also be used as a performance platform when drained.

→ The facades combine smooth surfaces that reflect the sky with modular units that pick up on the play of shadows as the sun moves across the sky.

← Composed of various types of textured concrete, the center is heavy in nature, almost as if it has been carved out of its corner plot, rather than deposited on it.

→   In many ways, that move has defined Neri&Hu as a studio, and they now employ around 100 architects, product designers, interior designers, and graphic designers. Rossana Hu, who is generally calmer and more measured when speaking than her often impassioned husband, is analytical when attempting to define the identity of Neri&Hu: "I think there are two different groups here that identify us kind of differently." She explains that while the local professional architecture community probably saw the duo as "American-trained, Chinese diasporic architects who are returnees," the design media has generally embraced the studio as almost representing a local voice. Neri tends to agree: "It was hard for Chinese architects to accept us, as they think we are foreigners, and yet that goes for a lot of Americans too, who might think 'they're Chinese, they're really not American.'"

For Neri, however, cultural identity is irrelevant when confronted with the issue of quality. "Even if you are born, bred, and educated in China, the Chinese will not want you to join them if you are doing bad work." And aiming, as they do, for the top-end clients in the market, Neri&Hu have indeed become known for the exacting finish, aesthetic, and material harmony that usually comes with a big budget. At the Aranya Art Center, completed in 2019, a cultural space was commissioned for a seaside resort community at Qinhuangdao by what the project literature calls the "enlightened developer." Drawing inspiration from the ocean nearby and the way it changes in texture and color through the seasons: from calm azure in summer to the splintered ice of winter, the use of concrete, aggregates, and other materials shows undeniable finesse. This gray-clad "box" for culture is a confident yet refined gesture for the community inside a beautifully proportioned amphitheater, one that recalls modernist brutalism or even ancient Neolithic spaces and demonstrates a deep commitment to the pursuit of the arts.

Neri points to another factor that might contribute to the Neri&Hu success story (the studio had 400 project requests in 2018, accepting only 15 of them), that of being a completely interdisciplinary practice. Long having had a finger in many pies, the studio deals with architecture, interiors, and graphic design, as well as lines of furniture and product design, to the extent that the early 20th-century German notion of "Gesamtkunstwerk" (total artwork) is   →

↑ Right from the entrance, fluted bronze walls reminiscent of theater curtains guide theatergoers into the building.

→ At the New Shanghai Theater, Neri&Hu marries a heavy, gray stone facade with exquisite bronze details to recall the glamour of the 1930s original.

↓ The theater entrance is set back from the sidewalk to provide a covered space in which passersby can experience the grandeur of the building.

↑ The minimalist internal courtyard at the Waterhouse hotel offers
a surprising contrast to the 1930 concrete facade (previous pages).

→ Neri&Hu were bold in their decision to leave areas of the Waterhouse
interior unrestored following a period of dereliction.

"I think architects today need to be able to express culture through the built environment, not just for the present, but to link the past with the future."
—Lyndon Neri

→ often used to describe this Shanghai office's output. At Neri&Hu, one quickly discovers, however, that this is not art and design simply for the love of it; on the contrary, from the very first days after they set the studio up, the couple branched out with the intention of increasing their business opportunities. "In China, often, you must be successful in a very short time," explains Neri alluding to the rapid construction times, which those elsewhere find mind-boggling. By taking responsibility for the totality of the design, from architecture to interiors, to furniture, and even graphics and branding, Neri&Hu often empower themselves in the process. "Tweaking the interior gives us the chance to make more tweaks to the architecture and so on," reveals Neri in his often charming, candid manner. "Being interdisciplinary actually helps us to buy more time."

The Waterhouse, a 19-room boutique hotel in Shanghai's South Bund district, was a watershed moment for Neri&Hu. It is an architectural concept that rests on the contrast between old and new, say the architects. The original structure was built as an army headquarters for the occupying Japanese in the 1930s, and the facade and structure feature Corten steel interventions while much of the original fabric remains exposed. Neri likes to recount the story that →

For the top-end clients in the market, Neri&Hu have become known for the exacting finish, aesthetic, and material harmony that usually comes with a big budget.

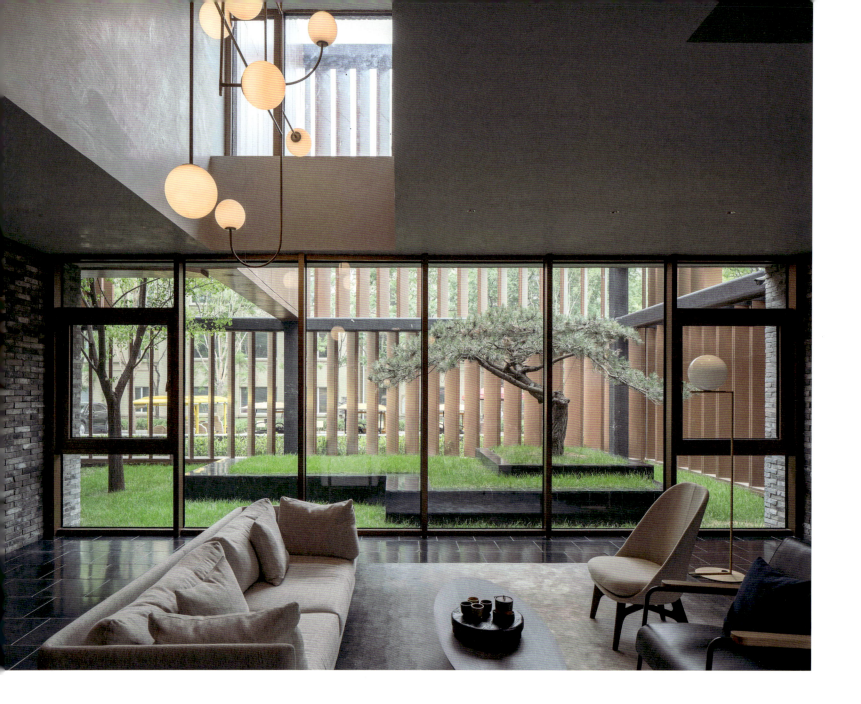

→ his own mother questioned whether the project was complete. It was unpopular at first, perhaps conveying too much honesty for the showy booming China of the time. Indeed, the Waterhouse, with its finely executed architectural rawness throughout, did not offer much appeal to a market with a taste for sleek metallic and glass finishes. However, the exciting juxtapositions, combined with the studio's masterful interior design, were bound to have its appreciators, and after a few years, requests and commissions started to pour in. "I think architects today need to be able to express culture through the built environment," concludes Neri with some parting thoughts, "not just for the present, but to link the past with the future." This deep respect for culture, both past, and present, is apparent in Neri and Hu's work and undoubtedly comes from their own story of "returning" to China. What Hu calls a "blurring of identification," has worked well for them. There is a feeling that wherever Neri and Hu find themselves, whether in New York, Shanghai, Singapore, or London, they tend to stand out, and in an increasingly competitive landscape, that can't be a bad thing. ∎

↑ At the Junshan Cultural Center, Neri&Hu transformed a donut-shaped office building into a clubhouse and sales center (previous pages). Within the building, all of the rooms are arranged in such a way that visitors are able to overlook one of several new outdoor spaces.

→ The new building for the Junshan Cultural Center has facades made from reclaimed bricks behind a skin of wood-effect aluminum louvers.

DESIGNER	New Office Works
PROJECT	Growing Up
LOCATION	Hong Kong

This New Addition to West Kowloon's Cultural District Takes Shape as a Timber Pavilion

This pavilion on the West Kowloon waterfront in Hong Kong was designed by New Office Works, who were commissioned to develop an informal temporary space. The structure, situated between the newly planted Nursery Park and the harbor, was designed to accommodate a range of public uses—from pop-up markets and workshops to small-scale events and performances—as well as serving as a place for people to congregate, contemplate, and shelter from the elements. The pavilion, constructed almost entirely from timber pillars and beams, is named Growing Up because it literally "grows up" from the southeast corner to the northwest corner, the timber pillars increasing in height from the rear of the pavilion to the front. In this way, the design reconciles the change from human scale at the rear of the building with the expansive scale of the waterfront. To emphasize this transition, the front and rear facades of the pavilion are open so that the building frames the view overlooking the harbor. Inside, a stepped area provides seating and a stage. With an eye on green features and sustainability, the pavilion's sloping roof incorporates a system of polycarbonate tubes and panels that channel rainwater into a pool surrounding the building. Although timber is rarely used on this scale in Hong Kong, it was an obvious choice when considering recyclability and the need to reduce the environmental impact when the structure is dismantled at the end of the project. ▮

↑ Peeping out of the roof of the pavilion, a palm tree acts as a landmark, signaling the location of the pavilion.

→ The architects resolved to keep the columns relatively slender so that visitors can weave easily between pavilion and park.

DESIGNER	HIL Architects
PROJECT	Meditation Hall
LOCATION	Cangzhou

Taking a Meditative Break from the Hectic Pace of Everyday Life

There is a deep sense of tranquility in the six former retail units that make up HIL Architects' Meditation Hall in the suburbs of Nandagang in Cangzhou, Hebei Province. The center, located on a busy commercial street with sprawling wetlands beyond it, is dedicated to activities such as Japanese tea ceremonies, the traditional arts of *kōdō* and *ikebana*, and yoga. Rather than demolish the original buildings and start again, the architects decided to retain the existing structural framework, but they reconfigured it to turn the focus inward, away from the street. At the heart of the building lies a vast meditation space lined with gold-toned wooden louvers arranged in a way that resembles fish scales. Very low-slung pendant lights accentuate the high ceiling and illuminate the room with a soft, mellow light, and the furnishings are sleek and sparse. A continuous walkway around the hall passes through a series of wood-clad corridors with stone paths elevated above channels of running water—a reference to the nearby wetlands. The sights and sounds of the outside world are muffled by thin steel membranes that cover the windows at the front of the building and cast beguiling shadows of the leafy plants growing outside onto the paving stones inside. The diffuse light bounces off the polished wood surfaces creating a relaxing warm glow. Cocooned in this way, the meditation hall is calm, quiet, and still—the perfect immersive and introspective Zen space for local residents to unwind and take a break from the hectic pace of everyday life. ▌

↑ Dried grasses remind visitors of the natural landscape beyond the hall.

← The walkway that surrounds the meditation hall reflects the gentle sunlight that filters in from outside.

↓ Within the meditation hall, artificial lighting has been used to highlight minimalist features of the design.

→ The low lighting creates a spiritual, immersive atmosphere for peaceful contemplation.

↘ At the far end of the hall, a window overlooking the trees outside offers a glimpse of the outside world.

↓ The hall's interior is sparse, the low-slung lighting emphasizing the vastness of the double-height space.

Amateur Architecture Studio

Sanhe Residence
(pp. 16–21)
Photography: Xia Zhi

Xiangshan Campus of China
Academy of Arts
(p. 168 top right)
Photography: Iwan Baan

Ningbo Historic Museum
(pp. 11, 286–289)
Photography: Iwan Baan

anySCALE Architecture Design

anyscale.cn

Wuyuan Skywells Hotel
(pp. 196–203)
Photography: Marc Goodwin (pp. 197–198, 202–203), Xia Zhi (p. 199–201)

Archi-Union Architects

archi-union.com

Inkstone House OCT Linpan Cultural Center
(pp. 174–179)
Photography: Tianzhou Yang (p. 175),
Tian Fangfang (pp. 176, 179),
Su Shengliang (p. 177–178)
Additional credits:
Developer: Overseas Chinese Town
Holdings Company (OCT Group)
Design: Archi-Union Architecture
Design Co., Ltd.
Contractor: Sichuan Yi Neng Da
Construction Engineering Co., Ltd.
Digital fabrication: Fab-Union
Architectural Technology and
Digital Fabrication Co., Ltd.
Landscape: Chengdu JZFZ Architectural
Design Co., Ltd.
Principal architect: Philip F. Yuan
Project architects: Alex Han, Xiangping Kong,
Huajian Gu, Hao Chen, Chuanshi Zhao,
Yuhao Fu
Interior team: Fuzi He, Ju Wang, Yifei Wang,
Luwen Liu, Jingyan Tang, Mengmeng Cui
Structural engineers: Zhun Zhang,
Tao Huang, Rui Wang, Zejiu Chen
MEP: Dawei Wei, Yong Wang, Ying Yu
Digital fabrication: Wen Zhang,
Xuwei Wang, Yong Peng, Yong Zhang,
Yancun Hao, Shengyang Xu
3D printing: Liming Zhang, Ce Li,
Liangliang Liu, Jie Zhang, Shilong Dai

ARCHSTUDIO

archstudio.cn

Organic Farm
(p. 130 right top and middle)
Photography: JIN Wei-Qi
Additional credits:
Design team: Han Wen-Qiang,
Li Xiao-Ming, Wang Han,
Jiang Zhao, Huang Tao

Twisting Courtyard
(pp. 8, 12, 188–195)
Photography: Wang Ning
Additional credits:
Chief designer: Han Wen-Qiang
Design team: Huang Tao
Furniture accessories: Song Guochao

Atelier cnS

ateliercns.com

Public Toilets in Zuzhai Village
(pp. 150–153)
Photography: Siming Wu
Additional credits:
Design unit: Atelier cnS/South China
University of Technology
Design director: Gang Song,
Guanqiu Zhong, Zhiyuan Zhu
Design team: Hairui Lin, Ruibo Li,
Zhongjing Xu, Tao Hu (intern)
Structure: Zimao Zheng
Construction unit: Dongguan
Huichun municipal landscape
Engineering Co., Ltd
Construction supervision: Xianggang Chun

Atelier Deshaus

deshaus.com

Long Museum West Bund
(pp. 13 bottom right, 230–231, 262–267)
Photography: Su Shengliang (pp. 13 bottom right,
262–265), Rory Gardiner (pp. 230–231, 266–267)

Atelier FCJZ

fcjz.com

Jishou Art Museum
(pp. 169, 172–173, 242–247)
Photography: Tian Fangfang

Atelier GOM

gom.com.cn

Longnan Garden Social Housing Estate
(pp. 26, 27 right middle)
Photography: CreatAR Images

Atelier tao+c

ateliertaoc.com

U-Shaped Room
(pp. 36–39)
Photography: Tian Fangfang

Capsule Hotel and Bookstore
(pp. 14, 138–143)
Photography: Feng Yuzhu (p. 14 top),
Su ShengLiang (pp. 14 bottom, 138–143)
Additional credits:
Furniture and lighting design: TIWUWORKS

AZL Architects

azlarchitects.com

Nanjing Wanjing Garden Chapel
(pp. 248–251)
Photography: Yao Li
Additional credits:
Cooperative Organization: Institute
of Architecture Design and Planning Co.,
Ltd. of Nanjing University

Shitang Internet Conference Center
(pp. 252–253)
Photography: Hou Bowen (pp. 252, 253 top),
Yao Li (p. 253 bottom)
Additional credits:
Cooperative Organization: Institute
of Architecture Design and
Planning Co., Ltd. of Nanjing University/
Shanghai Tongji Steel Structure Technology,Ltd.

Song House

(pp. 254–255)
Photography: Yao Li
Additional credits:
Contractors: Shanghai Yu Tong
Construction Group Co., Ltd.
Suppliers external wall: Shanghai He Tai
building materials Co., Ltd.
Suppliers interior wall: panDOMO,
Nanjing Bang Xi building
materials Co., Ltd.
Manufacturers: Shanghai Yu Tong
Construction Group Co., Ltd.

Bing Ding Wood Kiln
(pp. 256–261)
Photography: Yao Li
Additional credits:
Client: BingDing Wood kiln
Lead Architect: Zhang Lei
Design Team: Zhang Lei,
Zhang Xue

C&C Design

cocopro.cn

Heduli Paddy Hotel
(p. 134)
Photography: C&C DESIGN Co., Ltd.

Chinese University of Hong Kong/ Kunming University of Science and Technology

cpr.cuhk.edu.hk

Guangming Village Project
(pp. 131, 133 left top and middle)
Photography: Ce Wang

CROX International

crox.com.tw

Liyang Museum
(pp. 114–119)
Photography: Xia Zhi
Additional credits:
Client: Suwan China Cooperation
Demonstration Area Construction Co., Ltd.
City cultural consultant
and system service design:
Shangyuan Academy
Design team: C.R. Lin, Darcy Chang,
Dr. Zheng-Hao Song, Yue Jiang,
Saunaam Yip, Tian-Ye Zhou,
Jia-Yi Zhu, Li-Dong Sun, Nicky Ni
LDI: Nanjing Yangtze River Urban
Architectural Design Co., Ltd.
Curtain wall design consultant: Schmidlin
Curtain Wall Technology Co., Ltd.
Brand: Hai Tai, Tai Shan, TOTO

DAS Lab

das-design.cn

Lost Villa Boutique Hotel
(pp. 58–65)
Photography: Schran Studio/
Su Shengliang
Additional credits:
Principal designer: Li Jingze
Design team: Janet, Xiang Guo,
Duan Jinjin, Lu Zhangyu
Owner: Ningxia Zhongwei Lost
Villa Hotel Management Ltd.

Design Institute of Landscape and Architecture China Academy

caaladi.com

Boat Rooms on the Fuchun River
(pp. 74–77)
  Photography: Aoguan Performance
  of Architecture
  Additional credits:
  Architects: Kai Wang, Tuo Jin, Jianzheng Zhou
  Project manager: Guangjie Yu
  Consultant of wood structure: Suyi Guo,
  China Modern Wood Structure Construction
  Technology Industry Alliance
  Interior designers: Pantianshou Landscape
  Design & Planning Co., Ltd.

DnA Design and Architecture

designandarchitecture.net

Tofu Factory
(pp. 128, 130 left top and middle, 136–137)
  Photography: Ziling Wang

Bamboo Pavilion
(p. 129, 135)
  Photography: Ruogu Zhou (p. 129),
  Ziling Wang (p. 135)

Emerge Architects

emergearchi.com

SINICA Eco Pavilion
(pp. 124–127)
  Photography: KyleYu Photo Studio

Herzog & de Meuron

herzogdemeuron.com

M+
(p. 233)
  Photography: Kris Provoost

HIL Architects

hilarchitects.com

Meditation Hall
(pp. 310–315)
  Photography: Bo Cheng, Siyu Zhu

hyperSity Architects

hypersity.cn

Cave House in Loess Plateau
(pp. 66–73)
  Photography: hyperSity
  Additional credits:
  Architect in charge: Yang Shi, Shojun Li

V House of Dashilar
(pp. 180–183)
  Photography: hyperSity
  Additional credits:
  Principle architect: Shi Yang, Li Shaojun
  Design team: Yang Ling,
  Zhang Guoliang, Yin Manyu

I. M. Pei

Suzhou Museum
(p. 235 bottom right)
  Photography: Mi Chenxing

J. C. Architecture

johnnyisborn.com

JCA Living Lab
(pp. 30–35)
  Photography: Kuomin Lee
  Additional credits:
  Lead Designer: Johnny Chiu/
  Nora Wang
  Designer: Marisa Cheng

KRIS YAO | ARTECH

krisyaoartech.com

Water-Moon Monastery
(pp. 268–273)
  Photography: Jeffrey Cheng
  Additional credits:
  Architect: Kris Yao
  Team: Hua-Yi Chang, Kuo-Lung Lee, Wen-Li Liu,
  Jen-Ying Kuo, Yvonne Lee, Chin Tai, Jun-Ren Chou,
  Yi-Heng Lin, David Chang
  Structural consultant: King—Le Chang & Associates
  MEP consultant: Majestic Engineering
  Consultants Inc.
  HVAC consultant: I. S. Lin & Associates
  Consulting Engineers
  Landscape consultant: CNHW Planning &
  Design Consultant
  Civil consultant: Sino Geotechnology, Inc.
  Lighting consultant: Chroma33 Architectural
  Lighting Design
  Contractor: Fu-Chu General
  Contractor Co., Ltd.

llLab.

lllab.net

San Sa Village
(pp. 144–149)
  Photography: Fernando Guerra I FG+SG
  Additional credits:
  Project investor: 2049 Group
  Construction team: San She Inn (Beijing)
  Cultural Management Co., Ltd.
  Construction drawings: China Electric
  Design & Research Co., Ltd.
  Civil engineering construction team:
  Yi Wang and his friends
  Interior construction team:
  Guobing Zhou and his friends
  Deepened landscape design:
  Shanghai Di Cui Landscaping Co., Ltd.
  Landscape construction team:
  Mr. Cai and his friends
  Furniture consultation: cdc |
  brandcreation (Austria)
  Uniform design/production: carpostudio
  (Portugal)

LUO Studio

luostudio.cn

Party and Public Service Center
(pp. 13 top left, 158–165)
  Photography: Jin Weiqi
  Additional credits:
  Designers (architecture, interior
  and landscape): Luo Yujie,
  Wei Wenjing
  Client: Yuanheguan Village Committee
  Construction firm: Hubei Yufeng
  Construction Engineering Co., Ltd.
  Construction supervision: Shiyan Hongchao
  Construction Engineering Supervision Co., Ltd.

MAD Architects

i-mad.com

Hutong Bubble 218
(p. 25)
  Photography: Tian Fangfang

Harbin Opera House
(pp. 108–113)
  Photography: Iwan Baan

MUDA-Architects

muda-architects.com

Garden Hotpot Restaurant
(pp. 120–123)
  Photography: Arch-Exist,
  MUDA-Architects
  Additional credits:
  Client: Xinhua Nufang Restaurant
  Chief architect: Yun Lu
  Design team: Yun Lu, Jiandan Xu,
  Qiming Sun, Xue Chen, Yixiu He,
  Xiaoqiao Liu, Dian Rong,
  Shangyun Zhou
  Construction supervision unit:
  Chufeng Architectural Decoration
  Design Co., Ltd
  Construction supervision team:
  Xianyong Wu, Fei Jiang, Wenjie Tang,
  Songlin Li
  Construction team: Hao Chen,
  Chuangui Zhou, etc.

Neri&Hu

neriandhu.com

Tsingpu Yangzhou Retreat
(pp. 290–293)
  Photography: Pedro Pegenaute (pp. 290–291, 293),
  Courtesy of Neri&Hu/Tsingpu (p. 292)
  Additional credits:
  Design team: Lyndon Neri & Rossana Hu
  (Founding Partners, Principal in Charge),
  Federico Saralvo (Senior Associate),
  Ziyi Cao (Associate), Fong Huang (Senior
  Project Manager), Sela Lim (Senior
  Architectural Designer), Zhao Lei (Senior
  Architectural designer), Callum Holgate,
  Leyue Chen, Valentina Brunetti (Senior
  Architectural Designer), Sean Shen,
  Xin Liu, Bin Zhu, Nicolas Fardet (Associate,
  product design), Yun Wang, Jin Zhang

Aranya Art Center
(pp. 294–295)
  Photography: Pedro Pegenaute
  Additional credits:
  Design team: Lyndon Neri & Rossana Hu
  (Founding Partners, Principal in Charge),
  Nellie Yang (Associate Director,
  Architecture), Ellen Chen (Associate &
  Project Manager), Jerry Guo (Associate),
  Utsav Jain, Josh Murphy, Gianpaolo Taglietti,
  Zoe Gao, Susana Sanglas, Brian Lo (Associate
  Director, Product Design), Lili Cheng

New Shanghai Theater
(pp. 296–297)
  Photography: Pedro Pegenaute
  Additional credits:
  Design team: Lyndon Neri & Rossana Hu
  (Founding Partners, Principal in Charge),
  Ziyi Cao, Tony Schonhardt, Lei Zhao,
  Fongwin Huang, Yifei Lu, Nicolas Fardet,
  Xiaowen Chen, Christine Neri,
  Siwei Ren, Haiou Xin

Waterhouse Hotel
(pp. 298–301)
  Photography: Pedro Pegenaute
  Additional credits:
  Design team: Lyndon Neri & Rossana Hu (Founding
  Partners, Principal in Charge), Debby Haepers,
  Cai Chun Yan, Markus Stoecklein, Jane Wang

Junshan Cultural Center
(pp. 302–305)
  Photography: Pedro Pegenaute
  Additional credits:
  Design team: Lyndon Neri & Rossana Hu
  (Founding Partners, Principal in Charge),
  Nellie Yang (Associate Director, Architecture),
  Jerry Guo (Associate), Utsav Jain (Associate),
  Ellen Chen (Associate), Zoe Gao, Wuyahuang Li,
  Josh Murphy, Alexandra Heijink, Hwajung Song,
  Lara Depedro, Jason Jia, Brian Lo (Senior
  Associate, Product Design), Xiaowen Chen,
  Mona He, Cindy Sun, Jacqueline Yam

New Office Works
newofficeworks.com

Growing Up
(pp. 306–309)
  Photography: Xu Liang Leon
  Additional credits:
  Client: West Kowloon Cultural
  District Authority
  Architecture: New Office Works
  (Paul Tse, Evelyn Ting)
  Structural consultant (competition stage 2):
  Buro Happold Engineering
  (Victoria Janssens, Christoph Tritschler)
  Roof cladding consultant (competition stage 2):
  Front Inc. (Evan Levelle)
  Structural consultant (technical design):
  Simon Pickard
  Main contractor: Sun Fook Kong
  Construction Ltd.

One Take Architects
onetakearchitects.com

Shelter · The Mirrored Sight
(pp. 154–157)
  Photography: Kang Wei
  Additional credits:
  Architect: Li Hao

O-office Architects
o-officearch.com

Lianzhou Museum of Photography
(pp. 280–285)
  Photography: Zhang Chao

OPEN Architecture
openarch.com

UCCA Dune Art Museum
(pp. 234, 235 top, 236–241)
  Photography: Wu Qingshan (p. 234, 235 top, 236,
  239–241), Zaiye Studio (p. 238)
  Additional credits:
  Principals in charge: Li Hu, Huang Wenjing
  Project team: Zhou Tingting (Project Architect),
  Wang Mengmeng, Hu Boji, Fang Kuanyin,
  Joshua Parker, Lu Di, Lin Bihong, Ye Qing,
  Steven Shi, Jia Han
  Local design institute: CABR Technology Co., Ltd.
  Lighting design: Tsinghua University X Studio +
  OPEN Architecture

People's Architecture Office
peoples-architecture.com

Courtyard House Plug-In
(pp. 23, 24 right top and bottom)
  Photography: People's Architecture Office (PAO)
  Additional credits:
  Principals: He Zhe, James Shen, Zang Feng
  Project team: Cui Gangjian, Chen Yihuai,
  Gao Tianxia, Jiang Hao, Lin Tianquan, Liu Qianqian,
  Sun Liming, Wang Wei, Zhang Minghui, Zhou Ying

Shangwei Plug-In House
(p. 24 left, 27 bottom right)
  Photography: People's Architecture Office (PAO)
  Additional credits:
  Principals: He Zhe, James Shen, Zang Feng
  Project team: Sha Jinghai, Lin Mingkai

Studio 10
studio10.co

The Other Place
(pp. 90–95)
  Photography: Chao Zhang
  Additional credits:
  Architect in record: Fanben
  Director: Shi Zhou
  Design team: Xin Zheng, Xiangtong Wu, Zixia
  Huang, Ming Tang (project assistant)

Studio Zhu-Pei
studiopeizhu.com

Jingdezhen Imperial Kiln Museum
(pp. 166, 170, 171 top left)
  Photography: Su Shengliang

SUP Atelier
supatelier.com

History Museum of Qifeng
(p. 169 bottom right)
  Photography: Courtesy of SUP Atelier

TAOA
i-taoa.com

Two-Fold Yard
(pp. 40–43)
  Photography: Tao Lei
  Additional credits:
  Design team: Tao Lei, Chen Zhen,
  Kang Bozhou, Li Jing, Zhang Jinghong
  Engineering: Team Li Yi
  Landscape and interior: TAOA
  Construction: Team Sheng Changwei

Urbanus
urbanus.com.cn

Quad of Gourd
(pp. 15, 184–187)
  Photography: Yang Chaoying
  Additional credits:
  Principal architect: Meng Yan
  Project general manager: Li Yali
  Technical director: Yao Yongmei
  Project architect: Li Jing, Li Yongcai
  Team: Fang Xue, Lu Jing, Liu Yu, Bernat Riera,
  Jin Chenjia (schematic design) | Li Yongcai,
  Wang Zhe (construction drawing) | Zhang Suyuan,
  Cui Yi, Wang Sijie (MEP)
  Collaborator (structure): H & J International, PC

Tulou Collective Housing
(pp. 22, 27 top left)
  Photography: Iwan Baan
  Additional credits:
  Principal architect: Liu Xiadu, Meng Yan
  Project Architect: Li Da, Yin Yujun
  Team: Huang Zhiyi, Li Hui, Cheng Yun,
  Huang Xu, Zuo Lei, Ding Yu, Wei Zhijiao,
  Li Jing, Wang Yajuan, Zheng Yan,
  Shen Yandan | Zhu Jialin (technical director)

Vector Architects
vectorarchitects.com

Seashore Chapel
(pp. 204–205)
  Photography: Chen Hao
  Additional credits:
  Client: Beijing Rocfly Investment (Group) Co., Ltd.
  Principal architect: Gong Dong/Vector Architects
  Project architect: Dongping Sun
  Design team: Yi Chi Wang, Zhiyong Liu, Yifan Zhang
  Site architect: Dongping Sun
  Structural & MEP engineering: Beijing Yanhuang
  International Architecture & Engineering Co.,Ltd.
  Structural consultant: Lixin Ji, Zhongyu Liu

Captain's House
(pp. 132, 133 right middle and bottom, 206–209)
  Photography: Chen Hao (pp. 132, 133 middle and
  bottom, 206–207), Xia Zhi (pp. 208–209)
  Additional credits:
  Client: Private Client, Shanghai Dragon Television
  Principal architect: Gong Dong/Vector Architects
  Project architect: Chen Liu
  Construction management: Dongping Sun
  Design team: Dan Zhao, Cunyu Jiang, Zhao Zhang
  Site architect: Zhenqiang Chen, Liangliang Zhao
  Structural & MEP engineering: China Academy
  of Building Research
  Structural consultant: Congzhen Xiao, Yixin Du

Seashore Library
(pp. 210–215)
  Photography: Su Shengliang (pp. 210 top, 211),
  Xia Zhi (p. 210 bottom, 213),
  Chen Hao (pp. 212, 214–215)
  Additional credits:
  Client: Beijing Rocfly Investment (Group) Co., Ltd.
  Principal architect: Gong Dong/Vector Architects
  Project architect: Chen Liang
  Site architect: Yifan Zhang, Dongping Sun
  Design team: Zhiyong Liu, Hsi Chao Chen,
  Hsi Mei Hsieh
  Structural & MEP engineering: Beijing Yanhuang
  International Architecture &
  Engineering Co.,Ltd.
  Structural consultant: Lixin Ji,
  Zhongyu Liu

Alila Yangshuo
(pp. 216–223)
  Photography: Su Shengliang (pp. 216–217, 219,
  222–223), Chen Hao (pp. 218, 220, 221)
  Additional credits:
  Principal architect: Gong Dong/Vector Architects
  Interior architect: Bin Ju/Horizontal Space Design
  Architecture design team: Bin He, Nan Wang, Chen
  Liu, Fangzhou Zhu, Jian Wang, Mengyao Xu,
  Xiangdonbg Kong, Yue Han, Zhiyong Liu, Bai Li,
  Peng Zhang, Xiaokai Ma, Liangliang Zhao
  Interior design team: Jinjing Wei, Yaocheng Wei,
  Hongming Nie, Luokai Zhang, Fanyu Luo,
  Wenjun Zhou
  Site architect: Liangliang Zhao,
  Peng Zhang/Vector Architects; Yingfa Li,
  Xipu Li/Horizonal Space Design

BEAUTY AND THE EAST

This book was conceived, edited, and designed
by gestalten.

Edited by Robert Klanten and Elli Stuhler

Foreword by Wang Shu
Translation from Chinese to English
by Yoko Choy Wai-Ching

Introduction by Yoko Choy Wai-Ching
Profile texts by David Plaisant
Feature texts by Junyuan Feng (pp. 20–27, 164–171)
and Alvin Li (pp. 126–135, 228–233)
Project texts and captions by Anna Southgate

Editorial management by Lars Pietzschmann

Design, layout, and cover by Stefan Morgner

Photo editor: Madeline Dudley-Yates

Typefaces: Gopher by Adam Ladd,
Traulha by Yoann Minet

Cover photography by Wang Ning for ARCHSTUDIO
Back cover image by Kang Wei for One Take Architects

Printed by NINO Druck GmbH, Neustadt an der Weinstraße
Made in Germany

Published by gestalten, Berlin 2021
ISBN 978-3-89955-872-2

For more information, and to order books,
please visit www.gestalten.com

Bibliographic information published by the
Deutsche Nationalbibliothek. The Deutsche
Nationalbibliothek lists this publication in
the Deutsche Nationalbibliografie; detailed
bibliographic data is available online at
www.dnb.de

None of the content in this book was published
in exchange for payment by commercial parties
or designers; gestalten selected all included
work based solely on its artistic merit.

Editor's note: Although much of the focus in this
book is on mainland China, several buildings are
presented to showcase the architecture of
Taiwan. These buildings are included to show
a broader view of Chinese architecture.

This book was printed on paper certified
according to the standards of the FSC®.

Mechanical and electrical consultant:
Sen Lin, Haijia Li, Fuliang Wei, Jiaorong He,
Yu Gao/Shenzhen JS M&E Engineering
Desing Co.Ltd
Lighting consultant: Albert Martin Klaasen/
Klaasen Lighting Design
LDI: Guilin Institute of Architectural Design Co.,Ltd.
LDI project architect: Jianmin Qin
LDI architects: Mu Yang, Yuanxin Lu
Structural engineer: Wenfu Zheng,
Bo Li, Xianzhong Zhou
MEP engineer: Dengsheng Lin,
Xiaoyan Lu, Jing Deng
Landscape designer: Qianbai Yu, Yingying Xiao
Client: Landmark Tourism Investment
Company Hotel Management:
Alila Hotels and Resorts

Changjiang Museum
(pp. 224–229)
Photography: Chen Hao
Additional credits:
Architectural/interior/landscape design:
Vector Architects
Design principal: Dong Gong
Project architect: Sun Dongping
Construction management:
Zhao Liangliang, Chen Zhenqiang
Site architect: Guo Tianshu
Design team: Chen Zhenqiang,
Zhang Kai, Ma Xiaokai, Jiang Yucheng,
Teng Xiao-tong, Zhao Dan
Structural & MEP engineering:
Beijing Hongshi Design Co.,Ltd.
LDI project architect: Zhang Cuizhen
LDI architect: Li Mo
Structural design: Xue Wei,
Zhong Zhihong, Tian Xi
Mechanical & electrical design:
Shen Juan, Hao Shufang, Zhang Jianxia,
Shi Kefeng, Li Yingping
Lighting consultant: X Studio, School
of Architecture, Tsinghua University
Client: Shanxi Qiandu Real Estate
Development Co.,Ltd.

Waterfrom Design
waterfrom.com

TEA Community Center
(pp. 274–279)
Photography: Yuchen Chao
Additional credits:
Design team: Nic Lee, Elvin Ke, Richard Lin,
Eugene Huang, Morgan Chen/Waterfrom Design
Decoration: Waterfrom Design,
Gravity Company
Client: Zhong Nan Group

Wutopia Lab
wutopialab.com

Eight Tenths Garden
(pp. 78–83)
Photography: CreatAR Images
Additional credits:
Chief architect: Yu Ting
Project architect: Ge Jun
Design team: Dai Xinyang
Construction drawings: Zhou Yi Lian,
Chen Guohua, Yang Xueting, Ma Xinyu
Interior: Fan Riqiao, Zhang Zhe
Landscape: Guo Wen, Ni Zhicha, Baoyu
Interior and landscape design consultant: Yu Ting
LDI: Shanghai DuJuan Engineering
Design and Consultants Limited

Interior design: ShangRuiYuan Building
Design Consultants Limited
Landscape design: Atelier VISION

Slow Yangzhou Xinhua Bookstore
(pp. 84–85)
Photography: CreatAR Images
Additional credits:
Principal architect: Yu Ting
Project architect: Huang He
Lighting consulting: Zhang Chenlu
Construction drawing: Yangzhou
Architectural Design & Research
Institute Co., Ltd.
Interior: Shanghai Aoshi Design
Consulting Co., Ltd.
Landscape: Shanghai Tonggou Architecture
and Construction Design Co., Ltd.
Curtain system: Jiangsu Construction
Holding Group Co., Ltd.

Plain House
(pp. 86–87)
Photography: CreatAR Images
Additional credits:
Principal architect: Yu Ting
Design team: Xia Nurong, Huang Er,
Song Mengjiao, Pan Dali

Paper House
(pp. 88–89)
Photography: Chen Jie, Zhu Chen
Additional credits:
Architects: Yu Ting, Zhu Chen
Client: Yu Ting
Construct: Zhu Chen, craftsman.
Support: Chen Haoru, Sun Tian
Decoration: Chen Jie
Costume: Mr. Youzhang

X+Living
xl-muse.com

Shenzhen Neobio Family Park
(pp. 96–97)
Photography: Shao Feng
Additional credits:
Chief designer: Li Xiang
Project directors: Ren Lijiao, Wu Feng
Customized furniture: XiangCASA

Chongqin Zhongshuge Bookstore
(pp. 98–101)
Photography: Shao Feng
Additional credits:
Chief designer: Li Xiang
Project director: Liu Huan

Hangzhou Zhongshuge Bookstore
(p. 99)
Photography: Shao Feng
Additional credits:
Chief designer: Li Xiang
Project directors: Liu Huan, Fan Chen

New Century Magic Hotel
(pp. 102–103)
Photography: Shao Feng
Additional credits:
Chief designer: Li Xiang
Project directors: Ren Lijiao, Wu Feng

Zhuyeang Greentea Flagship Store
(pp. 104–105)
Photography: Shao Feng
Additional credits:
Chief designer: Li Xiang
Project directors: Ren Lijiao, Wu Feng

Park Zoo Hotel
(pp. 106–107)
Photography: Shao Feng
Additional credits:
Chief designer: Li Xiang
Project directors: Fan Chen, Zhang Wenji
Customized furniture: XIANG

Zhaoyang Architects
zhaoyangarchitects.com

Zhu'an Residence
(pp. 44–49)
Photography: Jonathan Leijonhufvud
Additional credits:
Design team: Yang Zhao, Peigen Shang
Structure system: Concrete Bearing Wall +
Concrete Block

Sunyata Hotel
(pp. 50–57)
Photography: Jonathan Leijonhufvud
Additional credits:
Design team: Yang Zhao, Zhou Wu, Peken Shang
Furnishing design: Xu Cai, Guoping Lai
Concrete construction consultant: Du Qingshui
Construction
Client: Travelling with Hotel Management Co. Ltd.

Additional images by:
dbimages/Alamy Stock Photo (p. 10 top);
Imaginechina Limited/Alamy Stock Photo
(pp. 10 bottom, 28–29);
Stockinasia/Alamy Stock Photo (p. 197);
KIP, The Moment/Alamy Stock Photo
(p. 168 left middle);
View Stock/Alamy Stock Photo (p. 168 bottom right)